"Laurence Graham is not just an observer of
He outlines how the Christian Church adapt
she faced different circumstances. We hear the word 'unprecedented' often these days. Yet, as this book makes clear, we would be foolish to ignore the missional lessons from our past."
Pastor Nick Park, Executive Director, Evangelical Alliance Ireland

"As a British Nigerian Pastor, ministering in Ireland, I found Laurence's views on mission very insightful and relevant especially in the interesting time and season we are in.
The book underscores that there is an urgent need for the church to step up to the plate by thinking outside the box with innovative ideas that can be deployed in reaching out to lost souls, previous church goers and even people who have made up their mind not to be receptive to the gospel, through the various utilisation of hospitality which was typical of Jesus' approach during His earthly ministry. I therefore recommend the book to every soul-minded believer."
Pastor Esirigho Ofurhie, Redeemed Christian Church of God, Ireland

"Hope from the Margins is a fascinating journey through the panorama of church history exploring how Christians have shared and demonstrated the good news of Jesus Christ down through the ages. But this is not a history textbook. By pondering how the past can inform our present and future, Laurence Graham's timely and essential book draws from his years of experience of grassroots mission. Hope from the Margins is an inspiring and thought-provoking 'must read' for anyone passionate about finding authentic, contextualised approaches to Gospel ministry in contemporary Ireland."
Ruth Garvey Williams, Editor of VOX magazine

"Mission has and always will be the heartbeat of the Church. For history to be of benefit to future generations they must learn the lessons from it.
    In his book, 'Hope from the Margins', Laurence takes us on a journey from the early days of the New Testament Church to present day Ireland highlighting what has and hasn't worked.
    It is clear from every age that there is no greater influence to the mission of the Church than ordinary Jesus followers living "distinctive and attractive life-

styles before their family, friends and neighbours," showing how their faith impacts in every area of their lives.

He skilfully shares the pitfalls to be avoided and enough hope to believe we can rise to make a difference in our generation. My prayer for those who read this book is that they rise to that challenge and so fulfil the call of God upon His Church."

Pastor Trevor Hill, Team Leader, Plumbline Ministries Ireland

"If today's church in Ireland is to fulfil its mission, Laurence Graham argues that it must give closer attention to the church of the first three centuries than the church of the last three centuries. This is a brave, thought provoking and practical look at the mission challenges that lie ahead in Ireland."

Seán Mullan, Founder of Third Space

"We have many lessons to learn from the past. Given this, I was delighted to read this excellent book which has emerged from Laurence Graham's PhD work. In "Hope from the Margins," Laurence skilfully considers the situational context of mission in the early church, drawing out lessons for us to learn about mission from the earliest followers of Jesus and through the Roman period. Laurence's survey of mission extends beyond the boundaries of the Roman Empire. This enables him to introduce a wider geographical perspective, and also helps us to engage with some of the mission journeys of the saints and monks of the Celtic tradition. In his discussion of mission today, Laurence identifies some of the tension that has emerged in missional thinking between attractional and incarnational approaches. However, he also highlights how he has seen both of these approaches continuing to operate in areas of Ireland and the possibility this presents for future imaginative and creative missional practice. In his last chapter, Laurence puts before us the possibilities offered by reflecting on this journey before, through and beyond Christendom. He reminds us that God still calls us to join in with His mission and to follow where he would lead us.

The breadth of source material and secondary literature is an indicator of the depth of work Laurence has undertaken. However, that shouldn't put off the non-specialist: "Hope from the Margins" is accessible and thought-provoking for those who wish to deepen their knowledge and for those who have previously engaged in Church history or mission studies alike. I will be coming back to it again and again."

Rev Dr Janet Unsworth, Principal of Edgehill Theological College, Belfast

"I want to recommend this book because of its encouragement to become imitators of Jesus Christ. Also, this book is very clear about how the early Church understood their mission in serving God."

Bishop Amos Ngugi, Leader of Acts of Compassion Ministries

"In Hope from the Margins, Dr Graham attempts to identify methods of evangelism throughout the church's history making relevant application to the reality of Christianity today as it tries to re-orientate its mission in a secularised world marked by a radical individualism, hyper-relativism and unbridled liberalism.

For many, the Church today has a credibility problem. Its 'truth' has been both compromised and damaged. So, how does the Church move forward? Graham argues that the Church must readily let go of its place 'of power in society', let go of its monuments, let go of its imperial impulses.

Graham is persuasive when he articulates that evangelism methods perhaps lie in the simplest of behaviours, such as hospitality, the personal invitation and use of language that communicates, respect, care, inclusivity, understanding and compassion that can lead a person to faith in Jesus and 'belonging' to the community of faith.

There are many reasons for recommending this book – the historical narrative is lucid and accessible. The treatment of how 'mission' and 'methodology' adapted in various historical, religious, social and political contexts and its application to evangelism today, is honest and thought provoking.

Hope from the Margins deserves to be widely read by Christians but especially those called to proclaim to a fragile and disorientated world the kerygma, the joyful announcement that Jesus Christ is a living Person to be encountered, who through his Resurrection has defeated sin and death."

Fr Kieran McDermott, Administrator of St Mary's Pro-Cathedral, Dublin and for ten years Director of the Diocesan Office for Evangelisation and Ecumenism

"The Church of Christ, especially in the West today is, like the church in the first three centuries after Christ, on the margins. This is an undeniable fact which Dr Graham convincingly illustrates in this book. We are where we are after a long period of what seemed like a hay day – a period when the Church and State operated in tandem, affording the Church the social and political power it did not have in the first three centuries of its existence.

Dr Graham reminds us that, on the margins, the church has all the challenges of the church in the first three centuries: small in numbers, having a life transforming message, with limited means. Those challenges offer us the same opportunity they offered the early church

The unique strength of this book lies in the suggestions he proffers as to the way forward, 'Irish solutions to Irish problems', is the best way to describe them, and each of them born out of his experience of mission in this country over the last two decades.

This is a book that inspires hope for Christian mission on this island and beyond, in circumstances that many seem to regard as increasingly hopeless. That hope is informed by solid research and experience, evidenced by the bibliographical references. Dr Graham reminds the Church of its call to live authentically. Authentic Christians, making a case for who they are by how they live and relate to those around them. No better way to evangelise the world!"

Rev Dr Sahr Yambasu. President of the Methodist Church in Ireland

"For anyone with a heart for Mission, this is a very worthwhile book. It researches the churches approach to Mission from the Apostolic period up to the present day. It also looks at the changing face of Ireland and considers how we need to adjust our approach to evangelism in light of these societal changes. Another value of this book is that Laurence has many years of coalface experience in ministry and shares with us from that experience adding greatly to its value."

Pastor Paudge Mulvihill, Secretary of Aontas (formerly known as the Association of Irish Evangelical Churches)

"Dr Graham courageously argues that the church has gone full circle in its missional self-understanding when we compare critically the first three centuries with our current century - but with nuanced differences.

Rightly critical of establishment fantasies, as a practitioner of The Word, he draws our attention back to lifestyle as the inspiration of mission now as then even more than strategies.

Dr Graham writes cogently, compassionately and confidently, bringing the early centuries of Christianity, both within and beyond the Roman Empire, into the ambit of his analysis of Christian motivation and service.

He is not afraid to name and to grasp the thorny issues that remain unresolved for our generation both in the incarnational and transformative communities of the church and outside the self-limitations of church itself - with God as our inspiration and guide."

Most Revd Dr Michael Jackson, Church of Ireland Archbishop of Dublin

"I have known Laurence Graham since he was a child in Portrush, Co. Antrim. It was here that he first trusted Christ for himself.

I regard this as a most important book for our time. In one sense it is a work of history. But also, the author draws from his own missional experience to illustrate some of the challenges that face us today, and the possibilities being given to us by Christ. It is His message of hope and salvation we must share with people from every kind of background by showing His love and acceptance and the unity and love that we have found in him.

This book is of huge relevance and importance. We should be grateful to Laurence for sharing his sound learning and penetrating challenge to help us be faithful servants of Christ today in the power of the Holy Spirit."

The Very Rev Dr Godfrey Brown is Minister Emeritus of Ballycastle Presbyterian Church in Co. Antrim, and is a former Moderator of the General Assembly

Hope from the Margins
Church history informing mission today

Copyright © 2022 by Laurence Graham

Requests for information should be sent via e-mail to Praxis Press. Visit www.praxispress.ie for contact information.

All Scripture quotations, unless otherwise indicated, are taken from the Holy Bible, New International Version®, NIV®. Copyright ©1973, 1978, 1984, 2011 by Biblica, Inc.TM Used by permission of Zondervan. All rights reserved worldwide. www.zondervan.com. The "NIV" and "New International Version" are trademarks registered in the United States Patent and Trademark Office by Biblica, Inc.TM

Any Internet addresses (websites, blogs, etc.) in this book are offered as a resource. They are not intended in any way to be or imply an endorsement by Praxis Press; nor does Praxis Press vouch for the content of these sites and contacts for the life of this book.

All rights reserved. No part of this book, including icons and images, may be reproduced in any manner without prior written permission from the copyright holder, except where noted in the text and in the case of brief quotations embodied in critical articles and reviews.

Paperback ISBN # 9798414941958

Cover design by Adam Fleming
Interior design by Jonny Lindsay

Printed by Amazon

PraxisPress.ie

TO KAREN,

THANK YOU.

HOPE
FROM THE MARGINS

CHURCH HISTORY
INFORMING MISSION TODAY

LAURENCE GRAHAM

PRAXIS PRESS

Contents

Introduction - 1

1. Mission in the New Testament - 3

2. Mission from the End of the New Testament until the Rise of Constantine - 19

3. Mission in the Fourth, Fifth and Sixth Centuries within the Roman Empire - 43

4. Mission Beyond the Mainstream of Roman Society - 69

5. Mission Today - 95

6. Mission from the Margins - 115

Conclusion - 139

Acknowledgements

Firstly. thank *you* for picking up this book. I am not really a historian though the first four chapters may seem like only history. My first passion is mission and I hope you will see that the history has much to teach us about mission today.

Thanks be to God for giving me life, for showering me with grace and for inviting me to join in His mission.

Thanks to Karen, Hope, Paul and Samuel for teaching me, encouraging me, challenging me and loving me, while making me laugh and keeping me humble!

Thanks to my dear parents, wider family, friends, pastors, teachers and congregations of my youth in Counties Offaly, Donegal and Antrim, who have shared God's love with me all through my life. This book remembers the early Church shoulders on which we stand but I am also very grateful for the immediate shoulders on which I stand.

I also stand on the shoulders of so many Christians around the world. It is one of my greatest joys to have had the opportunity to meet with and learn from Christians who are living and witnessing in a wide variety of different countries.

Thank you to all the churches where I have been blessed to serve in Haiti, Antigua, Belfast, Cavan, Longford, Cork, Kerry and Dublin. I am so grateful for our "partnership in the gospel from the first day until now". (Philippians 1:5)

Thank you to my Tutor, Rev Professor Laurence Kirkpatrick and to everyone else who guided and assisted me through the PhD.

Thank you to the whole team at Praxis Press. This book would not have happened without you. I am especially grateful to Ruth and Fraser for all your guidance, not to mention the proofreaders who have opened my eyes to the use of commas! Any remaining mistakes in this text are mine alone. Also to Jonny who worked so hard on the layout, especially with all those endnotes and to James for such careful project management.

I offer this book with the prayer that it will help us who have met Jesus to be more effective in sharing Him with others.

Laurence Graham
Dublin, January 2022

Introduction

'We are a New Testament Church'. What does that mean?
'We do mission in the same way as the early Church'. Really?

How did the early church grow during its first six centuries? And, can the answer to that question offer help to guide the mission of the Church today in the Western world, particularly in Ireland?

This book summarises the content of my PhD Thesis entitled "An Historical Analysis of Early Church Mission Methods". But the PhD work was done part-time while I served as a Minister in the Methodist Church in Ireland pastoring congregations, promoting evangelism and planting new churches. So, while there is lots of history in the following pages, I also consider what this history can teach us about mission today.

I want to make the history accessible and to encourage reflection on that history. Lynda Neilands observes that, "In moving into the future, we deal with the past in different ways – wrestling with it, ignoring it or treating it as a source of understanding and inspiration"[1]. I hope to take the third option by treating the history of the mission of the Church in the first six centuries "as a source of understanding and inspiration".

In the first three centuries of its existence, the Church grew rapidly. The small group of Christians gathered in Jerusalem developed into a network of churches that extended across virtually the whole Roman Empire and beyond. Did this happen in a spontaneous haphazard way or was there a blueprint? As the Church developed in structure and organisation did they devise and implement a strategic mission plan? At the birth of the Church on the day of Pentecost, 3000 people responded to a sermon preached by Peter.[2] Did this set the pattern for the ongoing growth of the Church?

Commenting on Jesus' invitation to, "see the lilies of the field, how they grow",[3] Christian Schwarz notes that the word καταμάθετε (katamathete), translated "see" in this verse, in fact means "intensively study" or "observe".[4] We are not so much to study the lilies themselves, but rather, to study their growth mechanisms. This book is an attempt to do exactly that with regard to the mission of the early Church, exploring how the mission of the Church took place and how Church growth happened.

In 1949 Herbert Butterfield, Regius Professor of Modern History and Vice-Chancellor of the University of Cambridge, wrote, "We are back for the first time in something like the earliest centuries of Christianity, and those early centuries offer some relevant clues to the kind of attitude to adopt".[5] Butterfield was somewhat ahead of his time but I think he was right and this book is my attempt to explain why.

As we survey these early centuries of the Christian Church we will see that its position in society changed over time and, therefore, so did its approach to mission. Then, in the last two chapters, we will apply the lessons of this history to mission in Ireland today, exploring what guidance history can offer us on reaching people for Christ, now that the Church no longer occupies the place in society that it once did. Through this we will see that there is hope from the margins.

1

Methods of Mission in The New Testament

INTRODUCTION

Towards the end of their time together Jesus left his disciples in no doubt that they were to tell others about him. Each of the Gospels ends with some form of commission and, just before he ascended, Jesus promised them that they would be his witnesses "in Jerusalem, and in all Judea and Samaria, and to the ends of the earth".[1] John Drane points out that this would have come as something of a shock for the disciples. Judaism was not generally involved in overtly sharing its faith with others, although people were welcome to come into the synagogues or the Temple precincts to investigate for themselves.[2]

Additionally, in light of what had just happened to Jesus, it would be understandable for the disciples to be wary of raising their public profile. Even so, the rest of the New Testament and indeed the continued existence of Christianity shows that they took their commission seriously and this chapter will examine some of the methods that these first Christians used as they embarked on their mission. In doing so, it is important to remember that behind all methods of mission lies the work of the Holy Spirit and the prayers of God's people. So, while the focus of this discussion is on the methods the Church used in their mission, we should not forget that methods count for nothing if they are not guided and empowered by the Spirit of God.

The book of Acts paints a picture of the message of Jesus spreading out. This dispersal was geographic, beginning in Jerusalem and radiating across most of the known world, but there was also a social/religious spread which has been described as a crustacean shedding its shells one by one.[3] The first Christians were Jews, initially Hebrews, but soon to be joined by Greek-speaking Jews. After the persecution following Stephen's murder, the gospel spreads through Samaria amongst those who were of Hebrew background but not considered true Jews. By the end of Chapter 8 a eunuch, who was not a Jew but who had been to Jerusalem to worship, is baptised by Philip.

Then in Chapter 10, Cornelius is baptised. He was a God-fearer and so had accepted the monotheism and high moral and ethical standards of Judaism. Not long afterwards a church is formed in Antioch, a city of highly sophisticated, educated, Hellenistic pagans, while by Chapter 16 of Acts we see Christians in Philippi, a Roman colony of Latin-speaking pagans. By the end of his life Paul had travelled much of Asia Minor, Greece and on to Rome. This is where Acts finishes its account, although in his Letter to the Romans Paul records his aim to travel as far as Spain.[4]

THE MISSION OF THE CHURCH IN ITS EARLIEST YEARS

Immediately after Jesus ascended his followers returned to Jerusalem[5] and the mission really came to life on the Day of Pentecost when a large crowd "came together in bewilderment, because each one heard their own language being spoken".[6] As a result of Peter's subsequent preaching, 3,000 people were converted.[7] While Pentecost was a unique event, it is likely that there were numerous other occasions in these early days when someone preached and many were converted, but these have gone unrecorded. Acts moves straight to a summary paragraph describing the life of the early Church.

> *"They devoted themselves to the apostles' teaching and to the fellowship, to the breaking of bread and to prayer. Everyone was filled with awe, and many wonders and miraculous signs were done by the apostles. All the believers were together and had everything in common. Selling their possessions and goods, they gave to anyone as he had need. Every day they continued to meet together in the temple courts. They broke bread in their homes and ate together with glad and sincere hearts, praising God and enjoying the favour of all the people. And the Lord added to their number daily those who were being saved".*[8]

This last phrase suggests that everything in the previous five verses contributed to the growth of the Church. The apostles' teaching was paramount, but also important were the miracles they performed. In addition, the common life of the believers clearly had an impact. So, this summary statement suggests that, undergirded by prayer, there were three primary means through which the Church began to grow: preaching, miracles and lifestyle.

PREACHING AND MIRACLES

The miraculous healing of a crippled beggar attracted a large crowd with whom Peter shared the message of Jesus.[9] The believers' prayer after Peter and John's release offers an insight into their thinking and makes it clear that they were convinced of the need for a two-strand approach to fulfilling their commission. They firstly, prayed that God would enable them "to speak the word with great boldness" and secondly that He would stretch out His hand "to heal and perform miraculous signs and wonders".[10] They understood that the spoken word and action had to go together.

It was not long before official opposition intensified further and the apostles were arrested again.[11] In prison they were reminded through an angel that preaching was to be their priority. They were told to "stand in the temple courts and tell the people the full message of this new life".[12] Clearly their passion was unabated because, on their release, "day after day in the Temple courts and from house to house, they never stopped teaching and proclaiming the good news that Jesus is the Christ".[13] The Apostles clearly felt absolutely driven or compelled to preach. Even the Sanhedrin observed, "you have filled Jerusalem with your teaching".[14] This fervent desire to preach seems to be rooted in their personal encounter with Jesus and the resulting conviction that he was the promised Messiah.

After summarising the death, resurrection and exaltation of Jesus, Peter and the other Apostles affirmed to the Sanhedrin, "we are witnesses of these things".[15] No amount of persecution and opposition was going to stop them from preaching this message. Presumably, this passion to preach was based on the fact that their own lives had been so transformed that they felt they simply had to share the news. As Peter and John themselves exclaimed, "we cannot help speaking about what we have seen and heard".[16] The mission of the Church at this stage was not some carefully planned strategy but rather a spontaneous explosion as a result of transformed lives.

These early chapters of Acts also suggest that many people were attracted to the Christians because of their growing reputation in performing healing miracles. Acts 5:15 describes how large numbers of sick people were brought in the hope that they would be healed even by Peter's shadow. Note that Acts does not suggest that Peter's shadow actually did cause anyone to be healed, but clearly the expectation of healing amongst the crowds was so great that some came to believe that this was possible.[17] This does not necessarily mean that miraculous healings were the direct cause of people being converted to Christianity, but healings did cause people to listen to the Apostles and to look on them favourably.

Twice in three verses in Acts 6, "the Twelve" affirm that their priority must be "the ministry of the word".[18] They clearly believed that preaching was a key method of mission, a vital tool for the propagation of the news about Jesus Christ. Indeed, throughout Acts it is regularly stressed that the number of believers grew "because the ministry of the word continued unhindered".[19] In the early days of the Church's life it seems to have been almost exclusively the Apostles who preached this message, but within a relatively short time more and more Christians began to be involved in preaching to others.

The opening verses of Chapter 8 describe persecution breaking out after the death of Stephen which resulted in many believers fleeing the city into various parts of Judea and Samaria. "Those who had been scattered preached the word wherever they went"[20] but there is still no sense of strategy in the mission of the Church at this stage. There is no evidence of a mission plan being developed and then acted upon by the leaders. Also, it is clear that at this early stage the whole Church participated in its mission, not just the leaders or specialist evangelists. This not only applied to preaching but also to lifestyle – Acts insists that the communal way of life of members of the Church played a significant role in attracting people to Christian faith.

LIFESTYLE AND COMMUNAL CARE OF THE CHURCH

The verses in Acts 2:42-47 which were discussed above indicate that the early Church understood mission as not just a department of the Church, but rather, as fundamental to its whole life. These verses also give the clear impression that the Church did not engage in specific outreach events; the way they lived and operated attracted people.

The life of the early Christian community was quite transparent to the general population. Acts 2:46 mentions that they met together every day in the Temple courts while Acts 5:12 specifies that the actual meeting place was "Solomon's Colonnade", a public setting. Sometimes referred to as Solomon's Porch, it consisted of two rows of pillars on the east side of the temple mount area. People would be inclined to walk under the colonnades and this area was popular for public lectures and discussions.[21] We see then that Acts 2:42-47 and Acts 5:12-16 describe how, in addition to the preaching and miraculous healings offered by the Apostles, the lifestyle of the Christian community had an impact because it was lived out in public.

The end of Acts 2 also indicates that social barriers were being broken down in the fledgling Church as evidenced in particular by the fact that they all ate together. In the Ancient Near East table fellowship was especially significant as can be seen in the Gospels.[22] Jesus was often criticised for eating with people whom others would have excluded.[23] In this context then it is notable that the early Christian community had a more inclusive table than would have been normal for the times. Irrespective of income level or social standing, they all ate together.

Acts 2:44-45 further relays that the believers held everything in common, while making it clear that some of them would have been in need otherwise. Acts 4:34 then claims that there were "no needy persons among them". This care for the needs of poorer Church members would have made the community attractive to many. As Santos Yao depicts, "The Christian meetings in the temple courts and the joyful table fellowship in various households exerted an impressive evangelising influence".[24]

More evidence of this communal care is found in the early verses of Acts 6 which describe a daily distribution of food to widows. Although Acts 6:2 records that the Apostles prioritised preaching ministry, the passage also confirms that social outreach and care for the poor was to remain a key part of the Church's mission. While affirming their commitment to preaching, the Apostles demonstrated the seriousness with which they took this distribution by appointing a team to facilitate it.

Acts 9 records an example of the witness of an ordinary believer with no mention of a preaching ministry. Dorcas "was always doing good and helping the poor".[25] Her witness had a big impact on those around her so that, when she died, the widows whom she had helped were heartbroken and, when Peter arrived, they showed him the clothing that Dorcas had made for them.[26] Obviously this lady's Christian faith had had a positive influence on her neighbours and it is likely that, as a result, some of them became Christians. There probably were many more Christians like Dorcas in the earliest years of the Church's life who contributed to the attractiveness of Christianity by the way they lived and by the practical care they offered to those around them.

A NEW DEPARTURE

The early verses of Chapter 13 of Acts mark a threshold in Luke's account. The commissioning of Paul and Barnabas seems to be the first time that the Church took an intentional, strategic mission initiative. Up until this point the work appears to have evolved according to circumstances, but now a clear decision is made to send out two 'missionaries'. Luke presents this as the first time such a commissioning occurs, although he has already recorded the, apparently full-time, ministries of people like Peter, Philip and the men mentioned in Acts 11:20. There is no evidence that they were similarly commissioned, and indeed it is unlikely that they were because their ministries began in the days immediately following Pentecost when mission appears to have been spontaneous and natural.

However, it is likely that at least 15 years passed from Pentecost until the commissioning of Paul and Barnabas in Antioch.[27] The fact that a commissioning was necessary may demonstrate that the Church had become more established and so it had to commission 'missionaries' to travel. Therefore the question arises as to whether mission was then becoming something of a separate 'department' of the Church, in contrast to what was discussed in relation to Acts 2:42-47.

Having said that, we should not understand this to mean that mission and outreach were necessarily becoming less important. In sending Paul and Barnabas, the Church in Antioch was not sending out a 'junior team', but rather its two key leaders who had already ministered amongst them for at least a year.[28]

It is worth noting that the list of prophets and teachers at Antioch shows significant diversity. Barnabas was from Cyprus, Simeon's nickname of Niger may mean that he was a black man from Africa, while Lucius of Cyrene certainly came from North Africa.[29] Manaen had in his youth been chosen to grow up as a companion of, the then Prince, Herod Antipas while Saul was a Pharisee from Cilicia.[30] Clearly the Church was straddling ethnic and social boundaries.

ASPECTS OF PAUL'S MISSION AS RECORDED IN ACTS

The accounts of Paul's ministry continue to paint a picture of both word and action being important in introducing others to the good news of Christ. On the island of Cyprus, Paul and Barnabas preached to the Proconsul but it was the miraculous blinding of Elymas the sorcerer which finally convinced the him. When he "saw what had happened, he believed, for he was amazed at the teaching about the Lord".[31] On the other hand, a little later at Pisidian, Antioch, there is no mention of miracles and it seems that the preaching alone had a big impact.[32] However, in Iconium, while they "spoke so effectively", the Lord also "confirmed the message of his grace by enabling them to do miraculous signs and wonders".[33]

In Ephesus there is a reminder that it was not just the 'professionals' who had an impact in leading others to faith. It seems that those who were converted quickly realised that their own lives had to change and they came openly to confess their involvement in sorcery.[34] The text specifies that this action of ordinary people had a powerful impact because "in this way the word of the Lord spread widely and grew in power".[35]

While describing his conversion, Paul makes it clear to King Agrippa that he understood God to have called him to devote his life to preaching the gospel. He said he was appointed by God "as a servant and as a witness of what you have seen of me and what I will show you".[36] There is no doubt that this commission burned passionately within Paul for the rest of his life. He travelled unceasingly at a time when travel was dangerous and difficult. Despite physical weakness, he constantly pushed himself. Paul describes his motivation as coming from a God-mandate: "Yet when I preach the gospel, I cannot boast, for I am compelled to preach. Woe to me if I do not preach the gospel!"[37] Still, in Paul's missionary work there is evidence of passion, clear-thinking and some strategy.

In the early part of Paul's mission, when he travelled with Barnabas and later with Silas, his visits to each place were usually quite short. It seems to have been his practice to appoint leaders as soon as possible after a new church community was established in a given location so that they could continue the work while he moved on.[38] In his Letter to the Romans, Paul writes that he has "fully proclaimed the gospel of Christ" from Jerusalem right round to Illyricum, continuing that "there is no more place for me to work in these regions".[39]

This would imply that once the initial establishing of the church was done, it was time for him to move on leaving others in charge of the Christian communities in each place. As Taylor describes, "In doing that, he was, in essence, planting the flag for God's mission in each province and thus establishing beach-heads that were both a sign of God's future and living examples of it".[40] Such a strategy meant that large areas were covered quickly and a church was established in key centres from which the message would spread to the surrounding area. 1 Thessalonians 1:6-8 appears to describe this strategy at work.

> *"You became imitators of us and of the Lord, for you welcomed the message in the midst of severe suffering with the joy given by the Holy Spirit. And so, you became a model to all the believers in Macedonia and Achaia. The Lord's message rang out from you not only in Macedonia and Achaia—your faith in God has become known everywhere. Therefore, we do not need to say anything about it."*

However, there is a frustrating lack of detail in these verses as to exactly how "the Lord's message rang out" from them to the surrounding areas. Did the Thessalonian converts travel or was it just the story of their response to the gospel which travelled? Note that Paul emphasises that it was not he or Timothy or any other of his associates who told others about the Thessalonians. They did not "need to say anything".[41] So it seems that "the report must have been carried by other people who, for whatever reason, travelled to neighbouring towns and even as far away as Corinth".[42]

Later in Paul's career his travelling strategy ceased on at least two occasions. He spent significant periods of time in Corinth and Ephesus but the geography of these two places probably explains why.[43] Corinth was located at one of the main 'crossroads' of the ancient world. It was at the land bridge between mainland Greece and the Achaean peninsula where ships travelling from the west were unloaded and their contents dragged across to be loaded onto other ships before continuing into the Aegean Sea. This was common practice because it saved a long and dangerous voyage around the coast. Also, many ships wintered in Corinth and so it has been estimated that there may have been an extra 10,000 people there during the winter months.[44] As a result Corinth had a rather transient population with many people staying there a short while before moving on somewhere else. So, for Paul, it was a place where people could hear the gospel and then take it elsewhere.

There was a similar situation in Ephesus which was the major port and administrative capital of the large Roman province of Asia Minor. In addition, Ephesus played host to many pilgrims because the main temple to the goddess Diana was located there. Paul spent well over two years in Ephesus and, again, it is easy to envisage people hearing him speak, encountering Christ and then taking the message either up country or across the sea. Thus we see that Paul's strategy in Corinth and Ephesus was to remain for a period in these cities while people from many places passed through, rather than him travelling to various locations on short visits as in the earlier years of his ministry.

When Paul arrived on the island of Malta, he found that, for the first time in his life, he could not speak the language of the people. He knew Hebrew, Aramaic, Greek and Latin but not Maltese and it has been suggested that this is why there is no record of a sermon preached on Malta.[45] This may be so, although it seems more likely that there would be someone in the group who could interpret. Nevertheless, communication through an interpreter is always more limited than direct communication. But, while no sermon is mentioned, Paul's mission continued through praying for the sick – preaching in action in a situation when preaching through words was perhaps more difficult than usual.[46]

The city clerk of Ephesus made a comment that offers some insight into Paul's preaching style. He reminded the people that, although Paul had spent over two years in Ephesus, he had not spoken against the goddess Diana.[47] It seems Paul's desire was to offer people a new way and let them draw their own conclusions about the old rather than engaging in criticism.[48] This substantiates his claim to be "all things to all people".[49] When considering Paul's preaching technique, it is important also to note that he appeared to realise the importance of two-way communication. We often see him engaged not just in monologue but in debate.

For example, the daily sessions which took place in the lecture hall of Tyrannus in Ephesus are described as "discussions".[50] The Greek verb behind this is διαλέγομαι (*dialegomai*) from which the English word 'dialogue' is derived. Luke chooses the same verb to describe Paul's approach in Athens both with Jews in the synagogue as well as in the marketplace.[51] Again, in Corinth the same word is used to describe his approach in the synagogue.[52] It appears that Paul frequently adopted this method to communicate the gospel.

The way that he preached varied according to his audience. For example, in the small rural village of Lystra, he illustrated his point using the cycle of the rain and farming practice, while in Athens, Paul's sermon was based on the standard rules of philosophy arguing the first principles of Christianity to an educated audience.[53] He did not have a 'one size fits all' message. Rather, he got to know something about his audience so that his presentation of Christ was contextual.

When Paul arrived in Corinth he met a Jew called Aquila who was also a tentmaker.[54] It is likely that this was no coincidence. When a stranger arrived in a city they could easily find out where immigrants from their own country were or where those who practised their own trade could be found "for these were the two most important factors in the formation and identification of neighbourhoods".[55] There is evidence that in many Roman cities ethnic groups tended to congregate in the same area and also, that people who shared the same craft or trade tended to work in the same zones. Based on this it is most likely that Paul's first contacts in a new city were his fellow tentmakers and their customers.

Historical sources indicate that workshops, such as those of shoemakers or leatherworkers, were recognised as a conventional social setting for informal discussion and debate. Given that,

"It is difficult to imagine Paul not bringing up the subject of the gospel during discussions with fellow workers, customers, and others who entered the shops – given the relative quiet of a leather working shop, given the many hours that Paul spent at work, given the utter commitment of Paul to gain converts for Christ".[56]

While this seems plausible, there is little hard evidence for it. There are hints to that effect in 1 Thessalonians 2:9 where Paul writes, "Surely you remember, brothers, our toil and hardship; we worked night and day in order not to be a burden to anyone while we preached the gospel of God to you", but this verse does not really clarify whether Paul preached while working or whether he worked at night and preached during the day.

Nevertheless,

"In the congested cities in which Paul lived, the high population density, especially in the parts of the city where someone of Paul's economic level could afford to live, meant that people were always around in a real sense, the urban shop functioned as a sort of neighbourhood coffee shop or ice-cream parlour where people could wander by, stopping for a few minutes of conversation, or linger to hear a teacher-missionary like Paul expound on the new thing he claimed God had done in Jesus".[57]

Such a scenario is highly likely, but the New Testament does not supply us with enough evidence to prove that the workshop played a major part in Paul's missionary activity beyond funding his sustenance.

GENERAL MISSION STRATEGIES OF THE NEW TESTAMENT CHURCH

Having looked at the strategies of the best known 'professional' missionary in the New Testament Church, it will also be helpful to identify trends in the strategies used by that Church generally.

Status

The first possible strategy to explore is the idea that early Christian missionaries purposely aimed at the conversion of a particular type of person or a particular level of society. Some of the members of the Corinthian Church appear to have been idolaters, adulterers, sexually immoral, thieves and drunkards,[58] leading many to conclude that the early Christian communities consisted of much the same kind of people who tended to be attracted to Jesus during his ministry on earth.[59] Indeed in the second century, the philosopher Celsus complained that Christianity claimed "everyone who is a sinner, a fool and a child...everyone who is in misfortune, him will the kingdom of God receive".[60] Moreover, we know there were slaves in at least some of the New Testament congregations.[61] However, it should not be deduced from this that there was an intentional strategy to reach out only to the poor or to the least respected members of society.

From the start people belonging to the upper echelons of society were a part of the Church too. As early as Acts 6:7, it is reported that some Jerusalem priests were converted and members of the priestly aristocracy in Jerusalem were often very wealthy.[62] Later, in Philippi one of the converts, Lydia, was described as "a dealer in purple cloth".[63] It has been estimated that a purple toga would cost approximately the equivalent of €60,000 today, so clearly she was a wealthy woman.[64]

In Romans 16:23, Paul conveys greetings to the Roman Christians from Erastus, the city treasurer for Corinth. Presumably he was a Christian. In the ruins of Corinth a stone has been found which had been on a large building and is inscribed, "Erastus. This was built with his own money not public funds". Certainly, he was a wealthy man. So there does not appear to have been a particular strategy to reach out predominantly to the lower strata of society.

Conversely, some have argued that there was a strategy to reach in the other direction. For example, Acts 13:6-12 records how Paul went to great lengths to ensure that an opportunity to share the gospel with the Proconsul of Cyprus was not jeopardised.[65] It may well be that Paul did prioritise such opportunities if they arose, not because certain people were of any more intrinsic value to God, "but their influence, if converted, was infinitely greater".[66] Nevertheless, Paul's underlying principle is spelled out in 1 Corinthians 9:22: "I have become all things to all people so that by all possible means I might save some" and an overview of what we know of his ministry and writings suggests that he "deliberately disregards the social and cultural classifications that were defined and maintained by the elites...The gospel concerns everybody; it needs to reach everybody, without concern for social, racial or educational boundaries".[67]

However, what was significant was that within the Church there was an effort to ensure that everyone would have equal status. Having already mentioned Lydia in Philippi, it is notable that the second convert there was a slave girl. Also, Paul's letter to Philemon asking him to be gracious to his runaway slave Onesimus would have been quite revolutionary in that age. Michael Green contrasts the letter to Philemon with an Egyptian papyrus where a slave owner writes to commission someone to go to Alexandria, find his slave and bring him to task.[68]

It is not clear how long such inclusivity continued but there can be no doubt that this crossing of barriers in what was a stratified society would have made the Church attractive, especially for those at the lower end of society. Having said that, it would probably have been much less of an attraction for people from the upper classes.

> *"A poor cabinet maker would certainly feel appreciated and honoured to call a prominent lawyer...his 'brother' and to be able to report that they were having a chat over dinner. If this lawyer would be asked by his friends where he had been the evening before, his story of having sat next to a cabinet maker on one side and a slave on the other side would have earned him only laughs".*[69]

Homes
Private homes played a huge role in the early growth of the Church. From the start they met in homes as well as in the Temple courts.[70] After Peter was miraculously freed from prison, it seems he knew to go to a particular home "where many people had gathered and were praying".[71] So too, private homes regularly acted as a venue for the preaching of the good news by invitation of the householder, such as the homes of Cornelius and the gaoler in Philippi.[72] The early Christians clearly made use of their own homes for the cause.

Aquila and Priscilla were quick to invite a theologically deficient Apollos to their home "and explained to him the way of God more adequately".[73] They also offered hospitality and a base for Paul during his first days in Corinth.[74] There is general agreement that the family/household was a basic unit of society in the Graeco-Roman world so that it was a disputed point as to whether the State or the household had first claim on a person's loyalty.[75] It is, therefore, not surprising that early "Christian missionaries made a deliberate point of gaining whatever households they could as lighthouses, from which the gospel could illuminate the surrounding darkness".[76]

Large tenement houses have been excavated under several churches in Rome. These places, where house churches would have originally met, seemed to have been comprised of shops on the ground floor with people living above. This is in keeping with what is known of common housing in the early Roman Empire where most people lived in large apartment blocks with shops on the ground floor facing the street, then manufacturing areas and living quarters over the shops and at the rear.[77] It has been estimated that over 90% of the population of cities in the Roman Empire lived in such tenement blocks which were called *insulae*. However, despite the archaeological evidence from Rome, it is unlikely that *insulae* were the most common venue for Christians to gather because the apartments in these tenement blocks were usually very small, often only a single room for a whole family. Therefore, it would be impossible to accommodate more than a few people at any gathering.[78]

It is much more likely that most Christian gatherings took place in a *domus* which was the type of home where wealthier people lived. These were large buildings consisting of a number of rooms clustered around a central atrium that were designed to house the owner, his family and all their household servants. Such homes were also built with social gatherings in mind and had a large dining room directly off the atrium. The atrium and dining room combined could often have accommodated 40 or 50 people. Furthermore, a *domus* was often, in effect, a semi-public building, given that the atrium was open air and located near the front of the house.[79] This helps to explain why Paul's letters often assume the possibility of "enquirers or unbelievers" coming into Christian services.[80] Situating the church in private homes made it easy for the Christian movement to spread naturally along family and social networks.[81]

Miracles

Another strategy issue which arises is the relationship between the spoken word and miracles. In the earlier parts of Acts, the continuation of the miraculous healings of Jesus' ministry through his followers made a big impression on the population of Jerusalem and beyond. This continued to play a part in Paul's ministry as well as that of other early evangelists. Paul spells this out in Romans 15:18-19 where, in the same sentence, he writes both of his speaking and also the power of "signs and miracles". Miracles probably played a larger role in the mission of the Church in these early years than in the subsequent centuries.

Lifestyle

In 1 Thessalonians 4 the Christians are urged to lead quiet lives and to work hard "so that your daily life may win the respect of outsiders and so that you will not be dependent on anybody".[82] Here is a clear exhortation to converts to use their ordinary daily working lives as a means of witness and mission. Turning to 1 Peter we read that the fundamental purpose of the "royal priesthood...holy nation" was "that you may declare the praises of him who called you out of darkness".[83] In order to do this they needed to, "live such good lives among the pagans that, though they accuse you of doing wrong, they may see your good deeds and glorify God on the day he visits us".[84] And again, "for it is God's will that by doing good you should silence the ignorant talk of foolish people".[85]

Paul called his communities of converts to be different from the world around them, but goes on to point out that their distinctiveness should not lead them to withdraw from normal society. So, for example, in 1 Corinthians 5:9-10 Paul clarifies that, in telling them in his previous letter not to associate with sexually immoral people, he did not mean the people of the world who are immoral or greedy because "in that case you would have to leave this world".[86] Notwithstanding the importance of moral purity within the Christian community, they are to be in the world.

Again, the instruction in 1 Corinthians 7 to a believing husband or wife to stick with their unbelieving spouse carries an explicitly missionary motivation, namely that the Christian partner may save their spouse.[87] Similarly, Paul's careful discussion of the rights and wrongs of eating meats offered to idols in 1 Corinthians 8-10 concludes with his affirmation that "I am not seeking my own good but the good of many, so that they may be saved".[88] Likewise, the instructions on the use of tongues in 1 Corinthians 14 are not just to preserve proper order in the church, but with an eye to what unbelievers would think.[89] It seems clear then that the leaders of the early Church were aware that the lifestyle and behaviour of ordinary Christians was an important aid to mission.

On the other hand, later sections of the New Testament suggest that the Christian way of living sometimes brought criticism and accusation rather than respect. 1 Peter 4:3-4 reads, "For you have spent enough time in the past doing what pagans choose to do – living in debauchery, lust, drunkenness, orgies, carousing and detestable idolatry. They think it strange that you do not plunge with them into the same flood of dissipation, and they heap abuse on you". It is likely that this abuse would have resulted from the fact that Christians had stopped taking part in what most of their contemporaries would have deemed normal social activities and they had thereby strained their relations with family, friends and neighbours.[90]

This social exclusivity was further emphasised as Christians withdrew from participation in the traditional religious cults of their cities. This had far-reaching consequences because travelling markets and fairs were often held in temple precincts and in conjunction with religious festivals. Therefore, a Christian would not take part in these if he or she took seriously the requirement to avoid idolatry. Similarly, to be a member of a social club or a trade guild would mean participating in religious rites in honour of the patron deity, which a Christian would have resisted doing.

The consequence of withdrawal from these activities because of their cultic association would have greatly limited Christians' participation in society and would most likely leave their neighbours feeling shunned.[91] We shall see that this deviance between Christian lifestyle and the norms of society continued to deepen in the subsequent centuries, but clearly it began to be noticeable in the later New Testament period. "As obedient children, do not conform to the evil desires you have had when you lived in ignorance".[92]

CONCLUSION

The New Testament paints a picture of the mission of the Church being facilitated by a combination of pioneer evangelists preaching to crowds and planting churches, as well as ordinary Christian people distinctively living out their faith in their immediate locality. The deep sense of fellowship and mutual caring within the New Testament Church would also have drawn people living in tough circumstances, while the unique understanding that even slave and free are equal in Christ must have made a big impact.

2

Methods Of Mission Employed by the Church from the End of the New Testament until the Rise Of Constantine

INTRODUCTION

In the period between the end of the New Testament (c100-120 AD) and the rise of Constantine early in the fourth century the Church grew both numerically and geographically. Leaders laid down foundational doctrines of Christianity, developed liturgies and established Church structures. But, also during this period there were intermittent times of persecution under the Roman Empire. These periods of persecution greatly disrupted the Church. Many Christians were martyred while others saved their lives by denying their faith.

These centuries saw heresies arising to challenge the Church. In particular, Gnostic thinking was a constant threat to Christian orthodoxy with its teaching of the need for 'gnosis' (special saving knowledge or enlightenment) to escape the corrupted material world. Montanism exalted martyrdom and emphasised asceticism as well as prophecy and tongues. The teachings of Marcion attempted to do away with all of the Old Testament and large parts of the New.

From the late first and early second centuries AD we have writings of Church leaders such as Clement, Polycarp and Ignatius. Justin Martyr and Irenaeus also wrote during the second century while, into the third century, Tertullian was prolific in his writings in defence of Christian doctrine. Origen was another crucial figure with numerous writings including sermons and commentaries on Scripture. Important writers of the late third century include Minucius Felix and Lactantius. Early church historians also covered this period, of which Eusebius of Caesarea is the best known.

However, despite this wealth of sources, these writers made little attempt to describe or explain how the Church grew. Their main concerns were to teach Christians and to argue against those whom they saw as a threat to Christian doctrine during these centuries of persecution and challenge. Nevertheless, the Church continued to grow, and we will explore how by analysing the methods of mission used during the second and third centuries.

MISSIONARY EVANGELISTS [1]

One of the key methods of mission used by the Church in the New Testament period was travelling evangelists. After the New Testament period there is some evidence that itinerant missionary evangelists continued to be a force in the spread of Christianity. Eusebius describes a succession of people who, "leaving their homes…took up the work of evangelists, eager to preach the message of faith to those who had never heard it".[2]

Origen quotes Celsus (an opponent of Christianity) who in the late second century wrote that "we see also those persons who in the market places perform most disreputable tricks, and collect crowds around them".[3] Origen himself claims, "Christians do not neglect…to disseminate their doctrine throughout the whole world. Some of them, accordingly, have made it their business to itinerate not only through cities, but even villages and country houses, that they might make converts to God".[4]

Some evidence of the continued existence of such mobile missionaries comes from Armenia, which is generally regarded as the first nation in which Christianity became the official religion. Sozomen says that this was as a result of a miraculous sign performed in the house of King Tiridates of Armenia by a missionary named Gregory the Illuminator.[5]

Even within the New Testament period, there was a move away from itinerant evangelists to a more settled ministry. The *Didaché* is often cited for its discussion of itinerant preachers[6] but their mission is to those in the Church.[7] Luke records Jesus instructing the 72 evangelists to eat and drink whatever they are given in the house where they are staying "for the worker deserves his wage".[8] This contrasts with the *Didaché's* assertion that if an itinerant stays three days he is a false apostle.[9] This is because the *Didaché* speaks of preachers travelling around the churches while Luke is describing travel in unevangelised areas.[10]

The notional opponent of Christianity, Caecilius, describes Christians as "a people skulking and shunning the light, silent in public, but garrulous in corners".[11] No doubt this is overly cynical but there is little evidence to suggest that travelling evangelists gathered large crowds in a public place to hear Christianity preached. In an environment where persecution could easily become a threat this becomes understandable, even necessary.[12] Travelling missionary preachers were not one of the main methods of mission in the second and third centuries.

Having said that, some clergy did fulfil the role of the evangelist/missionary. Ignatius, in his letter to Bishop Polycarp, challenged him to "exhort all men that they may be saved".[13] Certainly, it appears that Polycarp developed a reputation for evangelism as the multitude who accused him at Smyrna screamed, "this is the teacher of Asia, the father of the Christians, and the overthrower of our gods, he who has been teaching many not to sacrifice, or to worship the gods".[14] A generation later, Bishop Irenaeus clearly understood evangelism to be part of his role in that he learnt the Celtic language so that he could relate to the barbarians in the rural areas around Lyons.[15]

Another example of a missionary cleric is Gregory Thaumaturgos who was a native of Pontus but, when travelling through Caesarea, came in contact with Origen who led him to Christian faith. He remained under Origen's instruction for several years before returning home around 240 AD to become Bishop of his native city, a position he retained for approximately 30 years. His biographer records that Gregory "wished to see everyone converted from idolatry to the faith that saves…and eagerly searched all the cities and surrounding areas wishing to learn if there were any persons who had been deprived of the faith".[16] No doubt it is exaggerated rhetoric that on his accession to the Bishopric there were only 17 believers in the city while at the end of his ministry there were only 17 people who were not Christian.[17] However, for this rhetoric to be generated there must have been many people converted to Christianity under his leadership.[18]

During the second Christian century "the mobile ministry of apostles, prophets, and evangelists was beginning to give way to the settled ministry of Bishops (Elders) and Deacons".[19] On this basis some scholars argue that "in this kind of climate the missionary fervour of primitive Christianity would subside" further suggesting that the writings of this period "leave the impression of small self-contained socially stable communities concerned with their own good order and holiness, but having little regard for the outside world".[20] However, this overstates the case.

It is true that there was a huge reduction in 'professional' travelling evangelists in the style of Paul, but that need not lead to the assumption that the Church had lost its conviction of the need for mission and outreach. It is more likely that, as church communities became established, their methods of mission changed rather than their desire to be engaged in mission. For example, when Bishop Polycarp exhorts the Philippians to ensure that their conduct was "blameless among the Gentiles", it sounds like a Bishop urging his people to be blameless so that their lives would demonstrate the gospel and attract people to Christ.[21]

The fact is that the Church continued to grow despite a huge reduction in the number of itinerant evangelists and little evidence of high-profile preaching. So, rather than arguing that the Church lost its missionary zeal, it would be better to ask how mission was done if not by 'professional missionaries'.

THE APOLOGISTS

As well as the missionary clergy, another group of 'professional' Christians must be considered; those who argued for the faith through public disputation, educational establishments and in their writings. Teachers of philosophy were common in the Graeco-Roman world, so it is not surprising that Christians began to use this approach to convince others.[22] The apostle Paul used this method of mission in Ephesus, hiring the lecture hall of Tyrannus.[23] A few decades later Justin Martyr held classes for enquirers in a room over the public baths.[24]

Demetrius was Bishop of Alexandria from 189 to 232 AD. He was from a rural area and reportedly illiterate, but he opened the school of Alexandria which was to have a huge impact, particularly through its first three teachers – Pantaenus, Clement and Origen. The primary motivation may have been to combat the arguments of Gnostic Christians who said that Christianity was intellectually weak but such schools soon took on an evangelistic role.[25] Certainly, Origen saw his role as more than instructing those in the Church. He declared, "we do desire to instruct *all* men in the word of God".[26] Furthermore, Eusebius provides us with clear evidence that Origen saw his work as evangelistic. He records that some of the pagans who approached Origen were converted, including Plutarch who ended up as a martyr.

The written works of the Apologists were "the missionary literature of the second century, the presentation of the gospel to the pagan world".[27]

The *Apology* of Aristides is clearly evangelistic in intent because the author, having described that he himself has become convinced of the Christian faith, then writes, "And for this reason I was constrained to declare the truth to such as care for it and seek the world to come".[28]

Nevertheless, it is debatable how influential these works would have been in a largely illiterate world.[29] Still, that does not mean that we should conclude that the written Apologies were no asset to the mission of the Church because, even if they were only read by Christians, they would have provided information and arguments which Christian people could use in their witnessing to others.

Although a minority, some of those who came to faith did so on the basis of intellectual persuasion. The Apologist's work was essential in that it "assisted in the expansion of the new faith by providing necessary confirmation of its theoretical resilience".[30] The greatest contribution that the Apologists made to the mission of Christianity was that, in response to the criticism of opponents, they forged an intellectual basis for Christian belief even though they probably did not directly lead many people to faith.

PERSECUTION AND MARTYRDOM

It seems incongruous to think of persecution and martyrdom as a method of mission for the Church. However, persecution leading to martyrdom was something which reoccurred at various times during the first three centuries, so it is necessary to analyse whether this was a factor in the growth of the Church. Is there any evidence that the martyrdoms of Christians caused people to be converted? Certainly Eusebius, the most notable Church historian from that era, argues that they did. Having described some of the horrors of the persecution under Emperor Diocletian, he writes that, "In all these trials the magnificent martyrs of Christ were so distinguished throughout the world that eyewitnesses of their courage were astounded. They provided in themselves clear proof that the power of our Saviour is divine and ineffable indeed".[31]

Writing at least 150 years earlier, Justin Martyr also describes Christians being "beheaded, and crucified, and thrown to wild beasts, and chains, and fire and all other kinds of torture" and yet "the more such things happened, the more the others, and in larger numbers, become faithful, and worshippers of God through the name of Jesus".[32]

Similarly, Tertullian writes "the oftener we are mown down by you, the more in number we grow; the blood of Christians is seed".[33] But, why would the sight of Christians being cruelly tortured to death lead others into that faith? Pagan religion in the Roman Empire largely consisted of ongoing attempts to assuage the anger of the gods and, as a consequence, most people lived in fear of death without any assurance of a better after-life. In that context Tertullian argues that the obstinacy of Christians under persecution causes people to enquire about the basis of their confidence in the face of death. He goes on to claim, "who, after enquiry, does not embrace our doctrines?"[34]

Christians' response to persecution did sometimes have a positive impact on non-believers. Writing towards the end of the period under consideration in this chapter, Lactantius (c240-c320 AD) suggests that God permits persecutions to be carried out against Christians so "that the people of God may be increased" because "someone desires to know what that good is which is defended even to death, which is preferred to all things which are pleasant and beloved in this life".[35]

Justin Martyr describes his conversion both in his *Second Apology* and in *Dialogue with Trypho*. He implies that the impact of the martyrs played a part in his conversion to Christianity. "When I was delighting in the doctrines of Plato, and heard the Christians slandered, and saw them fearless of death, and of all other things which are counted fearful, [I] perceived that it was impossible that they could be living in wickedness and pleasure".[36] What he saw of the martyrs impressed him and was a step on the way to conversion by helping to confirm his growing intellectual convictions of the truth of Christianity.

Another example comes from Eusebius who gives an account that a soldier named Basilides led a Christian, Potamiaena, to her execution after she had been tortured. A short time later he was openly professing to being a Christian and was imprisoned. He testified that she appeared to him three days after her martyrdom and that this led to his conversion.[37] The *Martyrdom of Perpetua* also describes how Pudens, a soldier who was appointed as warden of the prison, began to "esteem [the Christian prisoners] highly".[38] A short time later it is recorded that "by now even the warden himself was a believer".[39] It seems reasonable to presume that he was converted because of what he saw in the Christians who were facing death.

So, the martyrs did have a positive impact on at least some non-believers and at least a few people were converted as a result of the martyrs, but it is important not to overstate the case as other people were put off Christianity for fear of what the authorities might do to them. Even Tertullian, in the same paragraph where he claims that "the blood of Christians is seed" notes that "we are counted a desperate, reckless race".[40]

The Emperor Marcus Aurelius criticised how ready Christians were to give up their souls "from an obstinate and peremptory resolution of the mind, violently and passionately set",[41] while Epictetus, a Greek philosopher, attributes the Christian martyrs' indifference to wives, children and the danger of death itself to "unreasoning regimen".[42]

As Rordorf summarises, "The witness of the Christian martyrs was received by the pagan world in two ways: with indifference and contempt, or with open admiration that could even lead to conversion".[43] The behaviour of the martyrs and the steadfastness of those who faced death had both a positive and negative impact on the growth of Christianity.

So, what was the impact of persecution on the Church itself? Writing in the middle of the fourth century, Basil of Caesarea wrote of the earlier centuries when,

> "the persecutors were manifest, and manifest too the persecuted. Then the people grew more numerous by being attacked. Then the blood of the martyrs, watering the churches, nourished many more champions of true religion, each generation stripping for the struggle with the zeal of those that had gone before".[44]

So, as well as claiming that the Church grew through persecution, Basil argues that persecution strengthened the faith and zeal of those already in the Church. Many scholars argue that, for the most part, the martyrdom accounts were written less to persuade pagans to convert to Christianity than to encourage Christians to strengthen their faith.[45]

In the second half of the third century the Church became more mainstream with increasing numbers of 'semi-Christians' as large numbers of people from all spheres of society joined the Church, or at least made some connection to it, without really becoming committed Christians. This was particularly evident during the decades of peace which the Church enjoyed after the death of Emperor Decius in 251 AD until the persecution initiated by Emperor Diocletian in 303 AD. So, "the third century church was both the church of a new Christian bourgeoisie, and a church of martyrs".[46]

Speaking of that time Eusebius writes, "greater freedom brought with it arrogance and sloth".[47] He goes on to describe how Church leaders began to attack each other and unity broke down, but then continues, "while the assemblies were still crowded, divine judgement, with its accustomed mercy, gradually started to intervene, and the persecution began".[48] The clear implication is that persecution was good for the Church in that it made it stronger and more united. As Vivian Green memorably puts it, the martyrs were the "athletes and warriors" of the Church.[49]

On the other hand, persecution could be detrimental to the Church in that it often led to schism resulting from different attitudes to those Christians who denied the faith under persecution. The Church in North Africa was particularly weakened by divisions over whether those who had buckled during persecution should be allowed back into the Church afterwards.

Hopefully, physical persecution and martyrdom will not be a mission method for the Church in the Western world, but modern history tells us that in parts of the world where Christians face persecution the Church is often strengthened.

MIRACLES AND EXORCISM

There is some evidence of miraculous healings and exorcisms continuing into these centuries. For example, in the Babylonian Talmud *Aboda Zarah* we are told Rabbi Ishmael warned his nephew Ben Dama not to allow himself to be healed by a Christian that came into the village.[50] This suggests that even opponents of Christianity believed that miracles of healing were being performed by Christians in the centuries after the New Testament.

Beginning with Justin Martyr and throughout the work of Christian writers of the second and third centuries there are regular claims that Christ has power over sickness and demons.

> *"And now you can learn this from what is under your own observation...our Christian men...have healed and do heal, rendering helpless and driving the possessing devils out of the men, though they could not be cured by all the other exorcists, and those who used incantations and drugs".*[51]

This is a big claim but Justin appears certain of its truth by saying that these things are "under your own observation". If Justin is prepared to challenge his readers to see what is happening, then it really must have been happening.

Origen, writing over a century later, speaks of the miracles done by the New Testament disciples before claiming that similar things continue amongst Christians up to his day, "They expel evil spirits, and perform many cures, and foresee certain events, according to the will of the Logos".[52]

Towards the end of the third century, Cyprian in his treatise *To Demetrian* describes in detail the power which the Christians have over demons and how they can exorcise them. He invites the reader to "come and learn that what we say is true".[53]

However, did the performing of miracles (or accounts of the performing of miracles) by the Christians lead to people becoming converted and joining the Church? Certainly, Irenaeus, claims that it did. In *Against Heresies* he writes that some Christians,

> *"Certainly and truly drive out devils, so that those who have thus been cleansed from evil spirits frequently both believe [in Christ], and join themselves to the Church. Others have foreknowledge of things to come: they see visions, and utter prophetic expressions. Others still, heal the sick by laying their hands upon them, and they are made whole".*[54]

Further evidence is provided by the author of *The Apocryphal Acts of the Apostles* who argues that miracles led to conversion. In 29 conversion stories in these documents, 22 of them describe how the performance of a miracle led to conversion. Nevertheless, it is important not to overemphasise the effect of miracles. There is an interesting passage in the *Apostolic Constitutions* suggesting that "all the ungodly are not affected by wonders".[55] So the writer concludes, "signs do not shame all into belief, but only those of a good disposition".[56]

Gregory Thaumaturgus, a Christian Bishop and miracle worker of the third century also seemed to understand this combination. In the *Life of Gregory Thaumaturgus*, it is recorded, that "his preaching greatly influenced the people" and that he "illumined the people by revealing God's power" so that people "were struck with wonder at the miracles he performed among the sick".[57] In the next paragraph we read that "they believed his words and actions came from God's power".[58] Later on there is a description of an outdoor meeting where Gregory "presented his teaching" before performing a healing miracle.[59] The clear picture presented of Gregory's ministry is that it was the combination of preaching and miracles which was so potent.

In his treatise *Against Celsus*, Origen responds to criticism that Christians who performed miracles were no different from those "who in the middle of the market-place, in return for a few obols, will impart the knowledge of their most venerated arts, and will expel demons from men and dispel diseases".[60] This charge reflects the fact that there were many 'wonder-workers' peddling their wares, often in an attempt to make money by generating awe amongst their spectators. In response, Origen argues that such people (whom he calls jugglers) only do their works for show and that,

> "There is not a single juggler who, by means of his proceedings, invites his spectators to reform their manners, or trains those to the fear of God who were amazed with what they see, nor who tries to persuade them so as to live as men who are to be justified by God".[61]

In contrast, Christian miracle workers will want to encourage those who are impressed by their miracles "to undertake the reformation of their characters".[62] A true Christian miracle worker will want people to be "more fully instructed by his word and character than by his miracles, as to how they were to direct their lives".[63]

There can be little doubt that the miraculous impressed people in a world of limited medical care and almost universal belief in and fear of demons.[64] Nevertheless, it is unlikely that it was a major factor in the growth of Christianity, especially given "the fact that *thaumaturgy* (miracle working) and *thaumaturges* (miracle workers) were common in the Graeco-Roman world in which Christianity came into being".[65] For example, Origen cites Celsus' account of the North African god Asclepius, "that a great multitude both of Greeks and Barbarians acknowledge that they have frequently seen…Asclepius himself, healing and doing good".[66] The role of miracles in the growth of the Church at this time should not be over-emphasised.

This chapter began with the discovery that by the time the New Testament period ended, there were very few, if any, travelling evangelists and no evidence that the Christian message was being shared in mass preaching events. Yet the church grew dramatically during the second and third centuries, how? We have discussed the limited effectiveness of the Apologists, of persecution and of miracles in drawing people towards Christianity. There must have been other factors causing the church to grow during this period.

CHRISTIAN LIFESTYLE

One of the difficulties in assessing the history of the early centuries of the Church is that most of our evidence comes from the writings of particular individuals. There is very little information about how most Christians lived and what they did because ordinary people do not tend to record their own lives. However, it is important that as much assessment as possible be made of the lifestyle of ordinary Christians "because otherwise we would see only a Church all head and no body, a phenomenon that affected only a few lives, a change without mass and therefore without historical significance".[67]

The Christians of the early centuries did not live in ghettos cut off from the rest of society. Tertullian assures all the citizens of the Empire that the Christians are "people who are living among you, eating the same food, wearing the same attire, having the same habits, under the same necessities of existence".[68] Inscriptions have also been found recording Christian butchers, woodcarvers, boat men, town councillors, lawyers, and even soldiers and athletes.[69]

Of course, Christians could not participate in everything as citizens in that they abstained from pagan religious observances.[70] There is also some evidence that more conservative Christians sought to maintain their identity in the Roman Empire by not attending parties in neighbours' homes, not sending children to public schools, refusing to witness athletic contests in the arenas or refusing to hold public offices.[71]

Still, most Christians did remain open to their neighbours and lived close enough to them that their lifestyle could be observed. So, did their lifestyle have a positive impact on these pagan neighbours? A number of sources suggest that it did. Athenagoras points out that,

"Among us you will find uneducated persons, and artisans...who, if they are unable in words to prove the benefit of our doctrine, yet by their deeds exhibit the benefit arising from their persuasion of its truth: they do not rehearse speeches, but exhibit good works; when struck, they do not strike again; when robbed, they do not go to law; they give to those that ask of them, and love their neighbours as themselves".[72]

Therefore, while the Christians kept apart and could not be involved in every aspect of the life of society, their way of living was obvious to their neighbours and friends. For example, it was evident that the sudden persecution under Decius was carried out by state officials with little cooperation from ordinary pagan citizens. So, it seems that,

"The old hatred with which Christians had been regarded was fast disappearing, together with the old slanders about their practices. The rapid growth in their numbers during the first half of the third century meant that most of the inhabitants of the Empire had Christians in the circle of their friends or their acquaintances".[73]

When Fructuoso, the Bishop of Tarragona, was being led to his execution in 259 AD, "the people began to sympathise with him, for he was much beloved of pagans and Christians alike".[74] This contrasts with the response of the crowd in the previous century at the amphitheatre at Smyrna who, when Bishop Polycarp was charged, "cried out with uncontrollable fury, and in a loud voice," that a lion should be let loose on him.[75]

Further evidence that Christians became more respected comes from the fact that, during the persecution under Diocletian in the early fourth century, a martyr at Edessa was clearly highly regarded because, "some of the Jews and pagans took part in shrouding and burying his body with the Christian brethren".[76]

A religion is often judged by outsiders according to the quality of living of its adherents and, if it can be shown to enable people to change their lives for the better, this can attract others and so be a method of mission. One piece of evidence that this was the case in the early centuries of the Christian Church comes from Origen who is clear that "the good deeds of Jesus have not been confined solely to the period of his tabernacling in the flesh, but up to the present time his power still produces conversion and amelioration of life in those who believe in God through him".[77]

At least a century earlier, Justin has enough confidence to challenge his readers to judge each Christian by their lifestyle.[78] He gives an example of a changed life in the wife of Urbicus. She had "formerly been intemperate" but, on her conversion to Christianity, her life changed and she tried to persuade her equally intemperate husband to follow her.[79]

In his *Octavius*, Minucius Felix makes big claims regarding the difference between Christians' way of living and those amongst whom they live. For example, while the pagans commit adultery, Christians are "men only for our own wives" and "from your numbers the prison boils over; but there is no Christian there, unless he is accused on account of his religion, or a deserter".[80] These claims may be exaggerated but there must have been some agreement by the opponents of Christianity that Christians lived admirable lifestyles or else the argument here would have easily been countered.

Cyprian's *Letter to Donatus* is thought to be his earliest work, written soon after his conversion to Christianity.[81] He describes how, before his conversion, he knew that to become a Christian would mean a change in his lifestyle and he struggled with how he would do it.[82] It is noteworthy that even before he was a Christian Cyprian knew that there was something distinctive about Christian lifestyle.

It would be wrong to give the impression that all Christians' behaviour was a good testimony to their faith. As the writer of *2 Clement* puts it, "when they see that we fail to love not only those who hate us, but even those who love us, then they mock at us and scoff at the Name".[83] However, on balance Christians presented a distinctive lifestyle which attracted non-believers resulting in church growth. Justin argues that people were converted because of what they saw in Christians. He speaks of former opponents "being overcome either by the constancy which they have witnessed in their neighbours' lives, or by the extraordinary forbearance they have observed in their fellow-travellers when defrauded, or by the honesty of those with whom they have transacted business".[84]

In his apologetic work *Against Celsus*, Origen writes of uneducated Christians who "often exhibit in their character a high degree of gravity, of purity, and integrity; while those who call themselves wise have despised these virtues, and have wallowed in the filth of sodomy, in lawless lust".[85]

Even opponents of Christianity recognised something good in the changed lifestyle of Christians. For example, the second-century pagan philosopher Galen writes that, "we have seen…those people who are called Christiani draw their faith from fables. Yet these people sometimes act in the same way as genuine philosophers do".[86]

The way Christians lived helped people to see that Christianity actually worked. As Frend puts it, "Gentile converts found in the ideal and sincerity of the Christians a practical fulfilment of the demand of the good life they had sought in vain elsewhere".[87]

Around the end of the third century the Neo-Platonist philosopher Alexander of Lycopolis, who scathingly described the philosophy of Christians as "simple", also had to admit that as, "the great masses hear these things [they] give themselves diligently to the pursuit of virtue and the stamp of godliness is set upon their behaviour".[88] Clearly Christian lifestyle made an impact on many outside the Church and thus was a method of mission aiding the growth of the Church in the early centuries.

For this reason Christian leaders quickly realised the crucial importance of Christian lifestyle. The *Didaché*, one of the earliest Christian documents, is most often referred to and quoted from for its instructions on baptism and its comments regarding travelling preachers, but the most striking aspect is in fact its teaching on Christian lifestyle. At the beginning this is made clear. "Now, the Way of Life is this: first love the God who made you; secondly, your neighbour as yourself; do not do to one another what you do not wish to be done to yourself".[89] It continues by spelling out some of the practical implications of this for Christian living.

Further evidence that teaching on the importance of lifestyle was important to early Christian leaders comes from Justin Martyr who, in his *First Apology*, spends three chapters detailing the moral teachings of Christ.[90]

The *Epistle of Barnabas* urges, "have among yourselves those to whom you may show kindness: do not forsake them,"[91] while *1 Clement* exhorts, "let us hasten with all energy and readiness of mind to perform every good work".[92] In his *Epistle to the Trallians*, Ignatius urges that their lifestyle be such that they give "no occasion to the Gentiles, lest by means of a few foolish men the whole multitude [of those that believe] in God be evil spoken of".[93]

Recognising that Christian lifestyle was key to the mission of the Church, Christian leaders made a point of teaching its importance. In a context of Christian worship services becoming increasingly private for fear of spies and informers, they realised that the way ordinary Christian people lived could have a big impact on non-believers.

This teaching began with new converts. Kreider argues that much catechetical teaching "seems to have concentrated on a re-shaping of the converts' behaviour".[94] He then goes on to describe the stages of conversion as recorded in the *Apostolic Tradition*. All through the process enquiry is made with regard to the behaviour and lifestyle of the candidates. "Have they lived good lives when they were catechumens? Have they honoured the widow? Have they visited the sick? Have they done every kind of good work?"[95] So Kreider concludes, "the new Christians might receive some private instruction by the Bishop about the sacraments that they had now experienced. But for them *the main task was to live as Christians*".[96]

By the time they were baptised, new Christians were trained and equipped to "do good works...and to conduct themselves rightly, being zealous for the Church, doing what they have learned".[97] This suggests that a key reason for such an emphasis on Christian lifestyle in the formation of new Christians was to ensure that the positive witness would continue.

However, no matter how impactful a Christian's life might be, at some stage there has to be verbal communication of Christ if non-Christians are to make the connection. So now we turn to consider how ordinary Christians also spoke of their faith to their family, friends and neighbours. In his reply to Celsus, Origen quotes extensively from the writings of this opponent of Christianity.

"See, indeed, in private houses workers in wool and leather, and fullers, and persons of the most uninstructed and rustic character, not venturing to utter a word in the presence of their elders and wiser masters; but when they get hold of the children privately, and certain women as ignorant as themselves, they'd pour forth wonderful statements, to the effect that they ought not to give heed to their father and to their teachers but should obey them; that the former are foolish and stupid, and neither know nor can perform anything that is really good, being pre-occupied with empty trifles; that they alone know how men ought to live, and that, if the children obey them, they will both be happy themselves, and will make their home happy also".[98]

Here is a vivid portrayal of Christianity being shared by ordinary tradespeople and unskilled workers talking freely of their faith to whoever will listen. Celsus pours scorn on a religion which is spread through such people but, in so doing, he gives us clear evidence that this was a means of spreading the faith.[99]

In 1857 some graffiti from the third century was found on the wall in the remains of the living quarters of the imperial pageboys on the Palatine hill in Rome. A picture depicts a boy standing in an attitude of worship with one hand raised up. He is worshipping a figure on a cross which has the body of a man and the head of a donkey. Written below are the words, "Alexamenos worships his God". The Jewish historian Josephus gives evidence that Jews were accused of donkey worship[100] and subsequently the same accusation was made against Christians causing both Tertullian and Minicius Felix to respond to the charge.[101]

This graffiti certainly suggests that one of the pageboys was well known by his colleagues as a Christian. Underneath is a second inscription written in a different hand saying "Alexamenos is faithful". Yarbrough describes and discusses this piece of graffiti in detail and concludes that "the target of the ridicule is worship of a crucified god".[102] Bryan agrees that whoever drew the graffiti saw the idea of a god dying on a cross as a joke.[103] Nevertheless, the fact that the graffiti was drawn at all suggests that Alexamenos is an example of an ordinary Christian making his faith public.

We must be careful not to exaggerate the level to which Christians in this period engaged in direct, intentional evangelism. As Latourette puts it,

> *"It would probably be a misconception to think of every Christian of the first 300 years after Christ as aggressively seeking converts. Such pictures as we have of these early communities in the New Testament and in the voluminous writings of these centuries warrant no such conclusion. In none of them does any hint occur that the rank and file of Christians regarded it as even a minor part of their duty to communicate their faith to others".*[104]

However, although there is very little evidence of organised evangelism that is not to say evangelism didn't happen because "many must incidentally have talked of their religion to those whom they met in the round of their daily occupations".[105]

One further piece of evidence that ordinary Christians did speak of their faith as part of their daily life is provided by the fact that the spread of Christianity often followed the trade routes of the Roman Empire and beyond. For example, Christianity appeared very early in Puteoli, which was on the Bay of Naples on the main route to Rome. When Christianity is first seen in Gaul it is in an area with which there was regular trade with the eastern part of the Roman Empire.[106] Similarly, there were Christians in Bautica in Southern Spain by the early fourth century, a region which was important in the trade of olive oil.[107] As well as merchants and tradesmen, many others travelled as part of the Imperial civil service or involuntarily as slaves or deportees.[108] It seems apparent that travellers who were Christian shared their faith as they went.

COMMUNITY LIFE OF THE CHURCH

Stephen Neill describes how, in the early years of the Roman Empire, there was a strong sense of community and mutual loyalty but that this sense of society quickly broke down. The Stoics tried to replace it by a wider loyalty with their doctrine of each person being a citizen of the world, an idea which was vigorously expressed by the Stoic Emperor Marcus Aurelius (161-180 AD). However, this theory was too remote to have much effect on ordinary people but, "What the Stoics had aimed at, the Christians seemed to have produced; here was a society in which all were welcome without distinction, from which the age-long discrimination between Jew and Gentile, bond and free, Greek and Barbarian, man and woman seemed to have been really banished".[109]

The second-century apologist Tatian described the Church of his day in similar language, "we do not make any distinctions in rank and outward appearance, or wealth and education, or age and sex".[110] Further evidence is provided by those executed with Justin in Rome in 165 AD. This was a diverse group of male and female, mostly free born but including one called Euelpistus who describes himself as a servant. They came from various places around the Empire such as Cappadocia and Phrygia as well as Rome.[111] It is notable that Perpetua who was "of noble birth" faced martyrdom while standing hand in hand with the slave girl, Felicity, so that "both of them stood as equals".[112] Two women from opposite ends of the social spectrum were united by their common faith.

At this time *hetaeria* (associations) became a common feature amongst craftsmen, artisans, merchants and shopkeepers. These people could not enter the social arena of the upper classes, although the wealthy often purchased their services. However, by forming an association such people derived a shared sense of belonging and provided each other with community and even friendship.[113] Normally these associations were for one particular group, perhaps of a certain trade, and that was the common link between them.

However, in the Church the common link was devotion to Jesus Christ and this could overcome all other potentially divisive classifications. The Christian community was different to *hetaeria* because it actively sought to include all types of people. This in itself must have acted as a strong attraction to Christianity for many people, especially those who came from the lower end of the social spectrum.

In his description of Christian meetings, Tertullian paints a picture of a mutual love and affection in the community, "one in mind and soul, we do not hesitate to share our earthly goods with one another. All things are common among us but our wives".[114] For Green this testimony from Tertullian is all the more significant because he wrote shortly after a mass turning to Christ in North Africa. So he concludes, "the quality of Christian fellowship to which [Tertullian] draws attention had had large scale effects in his native land".[115]

The closeness of Christian fellowship was clearly open to misinterpretation. The opponent of Christianity, Caecilius, quipped that the Christians, "love one another almost before they know one another. Everywhere also there is mingled among them a certain religion of lust, and they call one another promiscuously brothers and sisters".[116] This is exaggerated language in an attempt to defame the Christians but it does show that even opponents were aware that Christians shared a close and caring fellowship. The sociologist Rodney Stark has pointed out that Graeco-Roman cities tended to be socially unstable because they required a constant stream of newcomers moving into the city simply to maintain the population as the mortality rate was so high. Hence, "Graeco-Roman cities were peopled by strangers".[117] He goes on to describe the implications of this for society and cites evidence of social disruption in the cities of the Roman Empire before concluding that,

> "What does seem clear is that the social integration of Graeco-Roman cities was severely disrupted by the durability of internal ethnic divisions, which typically took the form of distinctive ethnic precincts. Ethnic diversity and a constant influx of newcomers would tend to undercut social integration, thus exposing residents to a variety of harmful consequences, including high rates of deviance and disorder".[118]

In such a context, the closeness of the Christians' fellowship and their commitment to each other, whatever their ethnic background and social class, must have stood out and surely would have acted as an attractive aspect of Christianity for many people. As Brown puts it, "the more poorly defined the family or social context from which new members come into a community, the more deeply they will be attracted by encountering a loving care that gives them a new identity or dignity".[119] The closeness of the Christian fellowship served as a means of growth for the Church, a method of mission.

The social cohesion and confidence of the Church community would have become even more attractive as the confidence and cohesion of the Roman Empire deteriorated. During these times of civil unrest, of corrupt and unstable government and of pressure from invaders around the borders, ordinary Roman citizens began to feel increasingly insecure. In contrast, Christians displayed a security which stood fast throughout any political and military ructions.

A tangible expression of the sense of community and mutual love which Christians held was their practical attention to those of their number who were in material need or other hardship. Christian leaders consistently taught of this necessity. The *Epistle to Diognetus* asserts,

> "Whoever takes upon himself the burden of his neighbour, whoever desires to benefit one who is worse off in that in which he himself is superior, whoever by supplying to those who are in want possessions which he has

received from God becomes a God to those who receive from him, he is an imitator of God.[120]

The command, in the *Shepherd of Hermas*, that Christians should help widows, orphans and the needy also extends to "rescuing the servants of God from necessities"[121] and Justin claims that "the wealthy among us help the needy".[122]

Evidence for this comes from a letter written by Bishop Cornelius of Rome in the mid-third century which mentions that the Church under his jurisdiction supports "more than 1500 widows and people in distress".[123] There is also some archaeological evidence of church buildings which had warehouses to store clothing and other items. For example, in Cirta, North Africa a large store of clothing was found containing 82 women's tunics, 38 veils, 47 pairs of women's shoes, 16 men's tunics and 13 pairs of men's shoes.[124]

This implies that the Church was a base for charity, although, as Wischmeyer points out, there are signs that this warehouse was to some extent a trading centre.[125] Clergy took a leading and increasingly co-ordinating role in this helping of the poor. In his *Epistle to the Philippians* Polycarp writes, "let the presbyters be compassionate and merciful to all, bringing back those that wander, visiting all the sick, and not neglecting the widow, the orphan, or the poor, but always 'providing for that which is becoming in the sight of God and man'".[126] Cyprian's biographer Pontius speaks of Cyprian as "distributing his means for the relief of the indigence of the poor"[127] and that "his house was open to every comer. No widow returned from him with an empty lap".[128] Even if this is exaggerated it does indicate that it was normal for Bishops to distribute help to the poor.

Slater discusses evidence that generous benefactors would hold public meals at which free food and even money was distributed.[129] Based on this Chadwick suggests that, as Bishops rose up the ranks of society, they adopted this model of charity so that at a Christian 'love feast' (fellowship meal) the poor would be well fed and perhaps even given food to take home for the next day.[130] Harnack cites an old legend of a deacon in Rome called Laurentius who, when asked to hand over the treasures of the Church during a time of persecution, responded that the poor were his only treasures. Harnack comments that "this was audacious, but it was not incorrect".[131]

Licinius, the Emperor in the eastern part of the Empire from 308 to 324 AD and who was behind the persecution of Christians, passed a law making it illegal to show kindness and supply food to prisoners. Anyone who did so would find themselves in prison.[132] This law was directly aimed at Christians and Harnack correctly points out that it "shows more clearly than anything else could do, the care lavished by Christians upon their captive brethren".[133]

Further evidence of Christians caring for prisoners comes from the pagan satirist Lucian who wrote *The Passing of Peregrinus* in which he depicted Peregrinus joining the Christians for a while until he was put in prison. When this happened, "the Christians, regarding the incident as a calamity, left nothing undone in the effort to rescue him. Then, as this was impossible, every other form of attention was shown him, not in any casual way but with assiduity…elaborate meals were brought in, and sacred books of theirs were read aloud".[134] Lucian's aim here is to poke fun at the Christians, but in the process he presents us with clear evidence of their generosity and of their care for each other.

Another aspect of mutual care was expressed in the burial of the poor. Lactantius writes, "we will not suffer the image and workmanship of God to lie exposed as a prey to beasts and birds, but we will restore it to the earth, from which it had its origin; and although it be in the case of an unknown man, we will fulfil the office of relatives".[135]

Tertullian claims that while the Christians did not spend money on frankincense to burn in the pagan temples they spent at least as much burying their brethren.[136] Knowing that the Church would cover funeral expenses would have been a comfort to poorer people and to their relatives and would have contributed to the attractiveness of Christianity.[137]

An additional feature of the community life of the Church was their caring for those of their number who fell ill. The *Canons of Hippolytus* highlight the attention which Church leaders are to give to those who are sick: "let there be a deacon to accompany the Bishop at all times, and let him point out to him sick persons severally. For it is a great thing for a sick person to be visited by the chief priest".[138] Also widows, who had probably received charity from the Church themselves, were involved in this ministry: "a special honour is to be paid to the widows on account of their frequent prayers, their care for the sick and their frequent fasting".[139]

Furthermore, the Church often sought to offer any necessary material help to those who were sick. The deacons were at the forefront of this ministry. Harnack notes that Cyprian's letters, which he wrote to the Church from his hiding place, are full of reminders to the deacons not to neglect the sick.[140]

However, it was not just the 'professionals' who were to be engaged in this ministry. As a letter of *Pseudo-Justin* puts it, "the sick are not to be overlooked, nor is anyone to say that he has not been trained in this mode of service. No-one is to plead a comfortable life, or the unwonted character of the duty, as a pretext for not being helpful to other people".[141] Again Tertullian's *Letter to his Wife* speaks of ordinary members of the Church "visiting the brethren...from street to street to other men's, and indeed all the poorer, cottages".[142]

In addition to caring for their own, there is evidence that Christian charity went far beyond the Church. Given Biblical mandates such as 1 Peter 2:12&15 it is not surprising that Christians offered help to poor and needy people.[143] In describing how the people make a weekly collection which is then left with the president of the congregation, Justin specifically mentions that it is to be distributed to "the strangers sojourning among us, and...all who are in need". [144]

Also, in the *Life and Passion* of Cyprian, Pontius says that Cyprian taught "that there was nothing wonderful in our cherishing our own people only with the needed attentions of love".[145] Evidence that this actually happened comes from the testimony of Pachomius who was converted early in the fourth century in Egypt. He had been press-ganged for service in the Roman army, but while he and others were in the gaol in Thebes the local Christians brought them food and drink. Pachomius, who had never heard of Christianity, asked who they were and was told "they were Christians, who were in the habit of doing acts of kindness to everyone, but especially towards travellers".[146]

Eusebius describes various occasions when churches reached out to help those who had been affected by famine or plague or other such disasters. Firstly, he records a letter written by Dionysius to the Bishop of Rome and his Church which states that, "it has been your custom from the beginning to show kindness to all Christians and to send contributions to churches in every city, relieving the distress of those in need".[147]

Eusebius also quotes from a letter written by another Dionysius, the Bishop of Alexandria, just after a terrible epidemic that swept across the region.

> *"Most of our brethren showed love and loyalty in not sparing themselves while helping one another, tending to the sick with no thought of danger and gladly departing this life with them after becoming infected with their disease. Many who nursed others to health died themselves, thus trans-*

ferring their death to themselves…they would also take up the bodies of the saints, close their eyes, shut their mouths and carry them on their shoulders. They would embrace them, wash and dress them in burial clothes, and soon receive the same services themselves".[148]

Dionysius continues that, "the heathen were the exact opposite. They pushed away those with the first signs of the disease and fled from their dearest. They even threw them half dead into the roads and treated unburied corpses like refuse in hopes of avoiding the plague of death".[149] People watching Christians treating the sick who had been set out on the street by their families must surely have been amazed and impressed.

Eusebius describes the actions of the Christians during the famine and plague which struck during the reign of Maximin (235–238 AD).

"In this awful adversity [the Christians] alone gave practical proof of their sympathy and humanity. All day long some of them tended to the dying and to their burial, countless numbers with no-one to care for them. Others gathered together from all parts of the city a multitude of those withered from famine and distributed bread to them all, so that their deeds were on everyone's lips, and they glorified the God of the Christians. Such actions convinced them that they alone were pious and truly reverent to God".[150]

Pontius, a deacon at Carthage, uses similar language in describing the actions of Cyprian and his Church during a plague there.[151] It is easy to imagine the impact that such sacrificial caring would have had on those who received it and on those who watched it happen. It surely must have attracted people into the Church.

Of course, the Church's social work needed funding and so, from the beginnings of the Church, Christians were called on to give money to support charity work. Justin describes what happens when the Christians come together for worship and Communion writing that, after the distribution of the elements, "they who are well to do, and willing, give what each thinks fit; and what is collected is deposited with the President".[152] This is then distributed to the poor and needy. Both the *Didaché*[153] and the *Epistle of Barnabas*[154] quote the words of Jesus that his followers should "give to everyone who asks".[155] Clement argues "better is fasting than prayer, and alms than both".[156] Similarly Cyprian writes to his people, "Let us give to Christ earthly garments, that we may receive heavenly raiment; let us give food and drink of this world, that we may come with Abraham, and Isaac, and Jacob to the heavenly banquet. That we may not reap little, let us sow abundantly".[157]

The context in which Cyprian wrote this is the plague which rampaged the Carthage area from 252 to 254 AD so it is understandable that he should encourage his people to give, although the tenor of his remarks suggest that he understood giving alms to be more for the good of one's own soul than as a witness to unbelievers. Nevertheless, the relief work done with these alms must have been a powerful witness.

At the head of Roman society was an upper class which was disproportionately small in number and yet was favoured by the law in all things. The rest of the population had very few rights at all.[158] So, there were plenty of marginalised people who needed charitable help. Furthermore, the general living conditions in Roman cities were atrocious. Stark has memorably tried to describe these as much as the evidence allows.[159] He paints a picture of astonishing population density and overcrowding which resulted in huge problems of sanitation with limited water supply and no such thing as soap. Additionally, there was no proper means of rubbish disposal so that even when it was not a time of plague, "illness and physical affliction were probably the dominant features of daily life in this era".[160] Therefore, mortality rates were elevated. Also, the rate of crime in these cities was very high and many people would have been cast into poverty as victims of crime. So, there were "extraordinary levels of urban disorder, social dislocation, filth, disease, misery, fear and cultural chaos".[161]

Hinson summarises,

"Christians astounded the ancients with their charity because, although Romans could be generous, they gave expecting some form of return in kind, at least in terms of honour and friendship. Furthermore, the Stoic philosophers regularly advised Roman people to single out the most deserving of their help. This meant that social aid rarely reached those who needed it most, at the bottom of society. This was precisely the people who the Christians aimed to help".[162]

It is easy to imagine that its social work made the Church attractive to many although there is relatively little hard evidence that this actually made converts. Nevertheless, it seems beyond doubt that the Church's charity work did draw people into their number. That certainly appeared to be the view of the apostate Emperor Julian (361 – 363 AD) who described Christianity as atheism. Referring to Christians, he wrote to Arsacius, the pagan High Priest of Galatia,

> *"Why do we not observe that it is their benevolence to strangers, their care for the graves of the dead and the pretended holiness of their lives that have done most to increase atheism?...The impious Galilaeans support not only their own poor but ours as well".*[163]

If an avowed enemy of Christianity claims that care of needy people both within and beyond the Church drew people to Christianity who are we to argue.

CONCLUSION

In the decades after the end of the New Testament, the itinerant evangelists and Church planters whose work was evident in the New Testament era seemed to have largely died out. Furthermore, there is virtually no evidence to suggest that the Church engaged in high profile evangelism during the second and third centuries. There are no records of large crowds gathered to hear a preacher such as is recorded in Acts. The key factors that influenced the growth of the Church during this period were the lifestyle of ordinary Christians, the community life of the Church and Christian care. People saw how Christians' lives were changed by their meeting with Christ and how they subsequently lived. Furthermore, people saw a very appealing Christian community and often benefited from its social outreach.

3

Methods Of Mission Employed by the Church in the Fourth, Fifth and Sixth Centuries within the Roman Empire

INTRODUCTION

Christians during the first three centuries of the existence of the church were usually a small, isolated and sometimes persecuted minority within Roman society. There was a clear boundary between those who were in the church and those who were not. Periods of persecution "inevitably established a clear line around the faithful community separating it from a visibly hostile world".[1] However, this changed radically in the fourth century as a result of the conversion to Christianity of the Roman Emperor Constantine at the Battle of Milvian Bridge in 314 AD. It is not at all clear that Constantine's conversion experience was genuine or had much real impact on his spiritual life, but he certainly identified himself with Christianity and this led to a complete turnaround in the religious climate of the Roman Empire. With remarkable speed, legislation was enacted which removed many of the previous restrictions on Christian worship and practice and within decades the law of the land favoured the Christian church even to the detriment of traditional Roman religious practices. So, from the fourth century onward the Church found that it was no longer an isolated, distrusted and even persecuted minority. In fact, during the years after Constantine's conversion, the church became increasingly mainstream until the point where it was counter-cultural not to be a Christian.

This change in atmosphere was warmly welcomed by the vast majority of church leaders and members. There was relief and even celebration that the pressure was off and there are records of Christian writers from that time clearly believing that Constantine had been sent by God to bring an end to persecution and oppression so that the church could function freely. Nevertheless, as history progressed it became clear that this was a mixed blessing.

The change in context also led to fundamental changes in the methods of mission of the church. Some of the means by which Christians attempted to reach out and encourage others into Christian faith continued, though with significant differences. However, as the civic authorities increasingly supported Christianity, a whole new set of opportunities and challenges arose for the church, resulting in the development of methods of mission which would have been undreamt of during earlier centuries. We will look first at methods of mission which continued into this period and then consider new methods of mission which arose in this changed environment.

The vast majority of the source material for this period comes from the hands of Bishops. They were the key leaders in the Church at this time and also played an increasingly important role in the administration of wider Roman society. The writings of Augustine, John Chrysostom, Athanasius, Ambrose of Milan and Basil of Caesarea take the form of sermons, letters or treatises on particular topics as well as Bible commentaries. Jerome, a priest in Rome, was also a significant theologian and historian. In addition, writers began to produce Church histories. The best known of these is *Ecclesiastical History* written by Eusebius, Bishop of Caesarea. Other important early Church histories were written by Socrates, Theodoret and Sozomen.

SOCIAL WORK OF THE CHURCH

The social outreach of the church certainly attracted people to Christianity during the pre-Constantinian period and it continued to be a priority for the church in the centuries after Constantine, but it changed in nature because, as the church grew, the scale of its social outreach work grew.

For example, the church at Antioch kept a list of 3000 widows whom it supported as well as regularly assisting prisoners, sick people, homeless people and injured people, while offering food and clothes to those who casually turned up at the church every day. In Caesarea, a hostel was built beside the church which was initially intended for pilgrims but ended up as a hospital for needy people. This soon began to receive funding from the

Roman Emperor because he recognised that the church hospital could help people more efficiently than the State.

Similarly, in Antioch the main church compound also contained a hostel for strangers and travellers as well as four dining halls to feed those who needed food. This level of social welfare provision was not just available in big cities. Serfass has studied papyri which "reveal that a well-organised charitable outreach" was also to be found in many small towns and villages in Egypt.[2] His studies reveal many insights into the scale and complexity of the Church's social welfare operation.

Increasing political instability brought a new category of needy person into the cities of the Western Empire. From around the 370s AD onwards Germanic tribes frequently crossed the Danube resulting in a flood of impoverished and homeless refugees in Northern Italy. The Church became well known for its care of such people so that in 408 AD the Emperor Honorius passed a decree placing formal responsibility for refugees in the hands of Bishops.[3]

The result of this vastly increased volume of social outreach activity was that it also became more institutionalised. Increasingly the church's outreach work was centred around separate buildings such as hospitals, hostels, dining rooms or orphanages. These large building complexes made the social work of the church more visible and increasing numbers of people in need were helped. But, as the social work of the church grew and became more institutionalised, it also tended to become increasingly separated from the evangelism of the church because the help was no longer directly linked with a worshipping congregation.

Of course, it is always a worthy task for the church to be helping people in need, but if this is done through a specialist institution then it is less likely to lead to the recipient being influenced towards conversion to Christianity. Much good was done and many people's circumstances were alleviated, but the direct link between the church community and its social outreach was weakened.

Pre-Constantinian Church leaders urged Christians to give towards the funding of social outreach work. Similarly, in the centuries after Constantine, preachers regularly challenged their congregations to give generously to help the poor. After noting that Paul ordered his churches to have a collection each week to help those in need in Jerusalem, John Chrysostom leaves his congregation in no doubt that they too should do likewise.[4] Indeed, John was often scathing in his challenge to the rich to give more. Once he accused them of paying honour to their excrements by using silver chamber pots! "It is you who should be ashamed, who are the makers of these things. When Christ is famishing, do you so revel in luxury?"[5]

As the Church attracted more and more people from high society, large donations increased to such an extent that sometimes even one donation could enable the establishment of a whole hospital or other institution. No doubt these large gifts enabled a huge amount of social outreach work to be done. They also possibly enabled those at the peak of the social spectrum to feel that they too had a place in the Christian Church. However, an inherent danger of this was that these wealthy leaders of society could have more influence on the work of the Church than perhaps they should.

Additionally, as the Church itself grew in wealth it came to own large tracts of land which again played a part in financing its work. By the time of Gregory the Great (Bishop of Rome c540-604 AD) the church in Rome was by far the largest land owner in Italy. The substantial revenue which these lands generated funded much of the Church's extensive charitable work.[6] "It may be said, in a word, that the Church did virtually everything that a large organisation with charitable interests would be expected to do in the face of poverty".[7]

MIRACLES

There is some evidence that miracles, or at least reports of miracles, continued to play some part in the mission of the Church and in attracting people to faith. One prominent example is the ministry of Martin of Tours (c316-397 AD), "the gift of accomplishing cures was so largely possessed by Martin, that scarcely any sick person came to him for assistance without being at once restored to health".[8]

Theodoret tells of a less well known example, a lady referred to as Mina in Iberia (Spain). Theodoret claims that the (unnamed) queen was healed through Mina's prayers, resulting in the Christian message being presented to her. She then took that message back to the royal household. Eventually the (unnamed) king agreed to build a church and contacted the Emperor Constantine requesting that Christian teachers be sent.[9]

Another example of conversions as a result of the miraculous is given to us by Sozomen. He claims that his grandfather and other ancestors "were converted through the instrumentality of the monk Hilarium" who expelled a demon in the name of Christ from one Alaphion whose "whole family, immediately embraced Christianity".[10]

Notwithstanding these examples, the role of miracles seemed to be decreasing. Speaking to Christian landlords, Chrysostom says "you cannot work miracles, and so convert them".[11] Similarly, Augustine (the Bishop of Hippo in North Africa) in a sermon based on Matthew 20:29-34 where Jesus healed two blind men, points out that, "Nowadays, while indeed blind flesh does not open its eyes at a miracle of the Lord's, blind hearts do open their eyes to the word of the Lord".[12] So clearly Augustine's view is that miracles are less prevalent now than they were in earlier centuries.

It appears then that fewer miraculous events were taking place at this time than earlier in the Church's history, although they did not cease completely. It also is noticeable that when miracles are reported they are generally on the fringes of the Empire and in clearly missionary situations.

APOLOGETICS AND OTHER EVANGELISTIC WRITINGS

During the fourth century and into the fifth, Christian apologetic literature continued to argue the case for Christianity and to answer pagan critics. One distinctive feature of apologetic writing after Constantine is that treatises were increasingly composed by clergy while in the first three centuries they were usually written by lay people.[13] By the middle of the fifth century, however, "the stream of apologetic literature had dwindled".[14] Of course engagement with pagans continued, but in many ways the great preachers of the Church replaced the Apologists.

Now that Christianity was legalised and often supported by the State, clergy such as Ambrose and Augustine had unconverted people listening to them in a way that would not have happened in the first three centuries of the Church. In addition, Church leaders engaged with pagan aristocrats through private correspondence.[15] Based on his studies of Augustine's literary corpus, Hinson concludes that it "reveals that he spent a substantial amount of time presenting the faith in a way which would appeal to the unconverted, conversing with interested persons, especially intellectuals and persons of note, and writing letters to answer enquiries or to defend and explain the faith".[16]

Augustine's own testimony makes it clear that Ambrose (Bishop of Milan c340-397 AD) had a great influence in leading him towards Christianity.[17] As Professor of Rhetoric at Milan, Augustine may have initially been attracted to Ambrose's sermons for their rhetorical standard, but as their content seeped into his consciousness he found many of his questions about the Bible being answered. Indeed, he was even impressed when he watched Ambrose at study. Clearly meeting a serious Christian academic had a big impact on this professor.[18]

CHRISTIAN LIFESTYLE

One aspect of the mission of the Church did not change with the conversion of Constantine. As Davidson summarises, "growth took place as much through personal contact, the sharing of experience, and the expression of practical Christianity at mundane levels as it did through formal proclamation or ceremony in the context of official Church activities".[19] But, of course, the bulk of this kind of mission must be attributed to nameless people whom we know little or nothing about. Ordinary Christian people telling their friends and family about Christ and demonstrating a Christian way of life is an effective way of introducing others to Christianity. It is reasonable to assume that this continued to be widespread, but we only have little snippets of actual evidence that it occurred.

One such piece of evidence is the poem by Endelechius Severus about three shepherds. Two of these shepherds, Buculus and Aegon, were downcast because their sheep were dying of a disease that was inflicting the whole area. They approached a Christian shepherd called Tityrus to enquire why his sheep were not dying. He explained that he was a Christian and that he had put the sign of the cross on the foreheads of his sheep. He went on to say that they too could have this faith and he referred to the words of Psalm 51:16-17 in telling them that God was not looking for blood sacrifices but for a broken and contrite heart. Buculus responded that if that is true then he would not hesitate "to join the true religion and leave behind the old errors". Tityrus responds that he is on his way to church so why does Buculus not join him, at which Aegon asks if he can also go.[20] Perhaps the details of the story are fiction but it is fair to conclude that the poet is giving an example of the kind of way in which Christians talked about their faith to friends and neighbours.

It appears that, in Jerome's experience, Christian members of a family could have an effective role in bringing other family members to Christian faith. In a letter to a Christian in Rome named Leata who longs for her father to come to Christ, he counsels her not to despair for his salvation, "for, when a man is surrounded by a believing crowd of children and grandchildren, he is as good as a candidate for the faith".[21] Such a concrete statement must imply that Jerome had seen this principle in action.

Augustine was also aware that the lifestyle of Christians could have the effect of drawing their friends towards faith in Christ. At the end of his sermon on the Samaritan woman of John 4, he notes that "many of the Samaritans from that time believed in him because of the woman's testimony".[22] Augustine continues, "so it is today with them that…are not yet

Christians. Christ is made known to them by Christian friends".[23] Nevertheless, Augustine acknowledges that, in his experience, the picture appears to be somewhat mixed. In another sermon he preaches,

> "Many bad things are done by bad Christians. Those who are outside and don't want to be Christians find plenty of ready-made excuses. When someone is pressing him to believe he will answer, 'Do you want me to be like that so-and-so and that one?...Sometimes too what he says is true".[24]

In his *First Catechetical Instruction*, Augustine warns that any candidate must be "put on his guard against those depraved persons who in mobs fill the churches in a bodily sense only"[25] but goes on to say that, "we should also assure him that he will find many good Christians in the Church".[26]

In previous centuries Apologists had pointed to the lifestyle of Christians as a means of attracting others to the faith. Now, Augustine realised that the behaviour of some Christians could in fact put people off Christianity. One of Augustine's main aims was to improve the ratio of worthy Christians to unworthy. To this end "he repeatedly exhorted Christians new and old to live lives that would be attractive and worthy of imitation – lives that would lure people into beginning the journey of conversion".[27] For example, he urges his listeners, "Be a good Christian and show up the pagans' stories for what they are".[28]

In a letter to Ascholius, Basil of Caesarea (330-379 AD) tells him that the account which he has given of the missionary beyond the Danube, Eutyches, has reminded him of "the good old times, when God's Churches flourished, rooted in faith, united in love, all the members being in harmony as though in the one body".[29] He laments that, in his situation now, the lifestyle of the Christian believers does little to attract people to the faith, "None of us now comes near Eutyches in goodness: so far are we from bringing barbarians under the softening power of the Spirit, and the operation of his graces, that by the greatness of our sins we turn gentle hearted men into barbarians".[30]

Throughout the fourth, fifth and sixth centuries Bishops, Catechists (teachers) and other preachers regularly urged their people to aim for a lifestyle which would attract others to the faith. For example, Cyril of Jerusalem's tenth *Catechetical Lecture* concludes with the exhortation,

> "You are called a Christian: be tender of the name; let not our Lord Jesus Christ, the Son of God, be blasphemed through you: but rather let your

good works shine before men that they who see them may in Jesus Christ our Lord glorify the Father who is in heaven".[31]

Similarly, Ambrose of Milan is concerned that his peoples' lifestyle would match their profession so that Christians might show Christ to others.

"Christ is the seal on the forehead, the seal in the heart - on the forehead that we may always confess Him, in the heart that we may always love Him, and a sign on the arm, that we may always do His work. Therefore let His image shine forth in our profession of faith, let it shine forth in our love; let it shine forth in our works and deeds so that, if it is possible, all His beauty may be represented in us".[32]

John Chrysostom also regularly called people in Constantinople to stand out from the crowd. However, he had an uphill battle – "the congregation vigorously applauded his oratory, but were reluctant to change their ways".[33] Nevertheless, Bishop John continued his struggle and in another sermon he exhorts, "Let us astound them by our way of life rather than by words. For this is the main battle, this is the unanswerable argument, the argument from conduct…Let us win them therefore by our life".[34]

Over a century later, in Gaul (France), Caesarius of Arles (c470–542 AD) clearly felt that ordinary Christian people had a big part to play in attracting others to the Church and he challenged believers to live lives that were "so just that Jews and pagans, according to the gospel: 'seeing our good works may give glory to our Father in heaven'".[35] They should also be ready to "clearly explain the mystery of the Christian religion to both Jews and pagans whenever there is an opportunity to do so".[36] Clearly Caesarius was aware of the missional implications of the behaviour of Christian people. He warned his congregations to guard their behaviour so that they would not put someone off from "being converted to God". [37]

While, in the centuries before Constantine the lifestyle of Christians was a major factor in drawing people to the faith, it became less effective subsequently. In fact, the way Christians lived could be off-putting to those considering the faith. But new reasons for Church growth emerged after Constantine which could never have been envisioned during the first three centuries of the Church.

SOCIETY PRESSURES

"Steady social pressures began to tell. The price of retaining honours, wealth and privilege was seen more and more to depend on accepting Christianity".[38] Increasingly it became the case that anyone with ambitions to rise up the promotion scale within the Imperial Civil Service would greatly enhance their prospects by making sure that they were seen to be part of the congregation of the Church. In Roman society those at the upper end of the social scale were usually the ones who took on leadership roles in public pagan religious rites. Many became priests while others acted as financial patrons. The result was that "as patron and priest, the upper class expressed and augmented their status and honour in Roman society".[39]

Christian Emperors and other Church leaders were aware of this and so, whilst State support was moving away from pagan institutions, attempts were also made "to assure those of high status that changing religion would neither deny them social esteem nor undermine the institutions upon which their social position rested".[40] For instance, opportunities for Christian patronage were created, whether it was the funding of the social outreach of the Church or financing the construction of large new Church buildings. For example, Salzman cites a substantial list of Roman aristocrats who funded the construction of Church buildings in and around the city of Rome. She also summarises archaeological evidence showing that aristocrats in the city of Aquileia acted as patrons of three basilicas which were built there in the late fourth and fifth centuries.[41]

In 383 AD a pagan senator Symnachus complained that some of his contemporaries were staying away from pagan altars out of ambition, "now to desert the altars is, for Romans, a kind of careerism".[42] So, Salzman concludes, "although pagan rituals and celebrations continued in Rome, there was a gradual turning away from pagan cults by urban elite aware of the mounting social and political liabilities in maintaining these traditions".[43]

In another study, Salzman conducts a detailed analysis of the literary epigraphic evidence relating to the Roman senatorial aristocracy. In particular, she assesses the evidence presented in *The Prosopography of the Later Roman Empire* which includes all aristocrats from 260-395 AD.[44] She finds that the rate of Christianisation varied over her period of study, tending to come in waves and that "these waves do coincide with the known religious preferences of the Emperors".[45]

She also found that, as the Imperial court became increasingly Christian, it in turn became "a Christian sphere of influence" so that "direct service to the Emperor in the Imperial court was a significant factor in favour of Christianisation".[46] This trend continued when the Imperial court moved from Rome to Milan where the aristocrats became Christians in large numbers because "Christian Emperors encouraged and supported co-religionists as courtiers and bureaucrats. It was advantageous, if one were an upwardly mobile provincial from Milan, to be able to attend Church services in the presence of the Emperor".[47]

Kreider notes that, when the Emperor Constantine converted, the Church required him to adjust his lifestyle. He compares this with the conversion of Volusian, a pagan Roman aristocrat, a century later. After a detailed analysis of his coming to faith over a long period, Kreider summarises: "for someone as 'distinguished and excellent' as Volusian, conversion would not require fundamental change in aristocratic behaviour".[48] In the early centuries of the Church, to become a Christian was a big risk and demanded an almost complete break with the norms of society.[49] It was to swim against the tide, but by the time of Volusian he "was being asked to ratify a social order, not to query it; to swim in the main stream, not in a cross current. But of course the main stream was now Christian".[50]

It can be debated as to what extent society merged into the Church or whether the Church changed to reflect society, but the fact remains that the two increasingly coalesced to become one, "the alternative society was becoming society itself".[51] It is difficult to quantify but increasingly 'herd instinct' must have come into play as Christianity became more mainstream in the Roman Empire. As MacMullen summarises, "If you were to notice that, recently, a good many of your comrades or neighbours were no longer attending the temple or that they seemed always to be attacking you for your own attendance, surely your comfortableness in your beliefs would suffer".[52]

In subsequent centuries if the 'herd instinct' did not work then the Imperial authorities were quite open to giving it a nudge. In 542 AD, the Emperor Justinian sent a Bishop and four deacons to convert rural areas of the four provinces of Asia, Caria, Lydia and Phrygia. 80,000 people were converted but each of them were given a sum of money sufficient to feed them for three years.[53] Thus, as the notables were converted so too were the masses but, as might be expected, many of these conversions were less than sincere.

Even Eusebius who welcomed virtually everything that Constantine did with unbridled approval, lamented the "scandalous hypocrisy of those who crept into the Church, and assumed the name and character of Christians".[54] It was now fashionable to be a Christian. As Jones puts it, "a more potent cause of conversion than calculations of material gain was the fact that Christianity became respectable".[55]

COERCION TO BELIEVE

At the end of his sermon on the parable of the Great Banquet, Bishop Augustine focuses on the instruction of the master to his servant to "go out to the roads and the country lanes and make them come in, so that my house will be full".[56] Based on this verse he speaks of the "heretics" of his day, "let them be plucked up from among the thorns. They have stuck fast in the hedges; they are unwilling to be compelled. Let us come in, they say, of our own good will. This is not the Lord's order, 'compel them,' says he, 'to come in'".[57] Augustine was by no means the first to advocate such action. Indeed, "almost immediately after having undergone persecution itself, the Church began to instigate the rulers of the world to persecute on its behalf".[58] This may seem surprising in light of the loving teachings of Jesus, but some Old Testament passages became influential such as Exodus 34:13-14 "break down their altars, smash their sacred stones and cut down their Asherah poles...for the Lord, whose name is Jealous, is a jealous God".[59] So, from the fourth century onwards coercion became a method of 'mission' of the Church. This coercion took various forms.

Beginning with Constantine, the Christian position was bolstered by means of legislation. Sozomen records that Constantine issued Imperial edicts which enabled "Christian men belonging to the palace" to remove all the valuables from pagan temples while "some were stripped of their doors, others of their roofs, and others were neglected, allowed to fall into ruin, or destroyed".[60] Before the fourth century ended laws were passed which explicitly forbade paganism, "If anyone should dare to celebrate sacrifices in violation of the law of our father, the deified Emperor, and of this decree of our clemency, let an appropriate punishment and sentence immediately be inflicted on him".[61]

Again, in 391 AD the law declared that,

"No person shall pollute himself with sacrificial animals; no person shall slaughter an innocent victim; no person shall approach the shrines, shall wander through the temples, or revere the images formed by mortal labour, lest he become guilty by divine and human laws".[62]

It is uncertain to what extent these laws were enforced, or even whether the bulk of the population was aware of them, but the general trend is clear – the law was increasingly being used to persuade or even force people towards Christianity. The leaders of the Church often encouraged this.

In 382 AD, the Emperor Gratian removed the Altar of Victory from the Senate building. However, a year later the more liberal Imperial regime of Justina and Valentinian II succeeded Gratian. Symmachus became the prefect of Rome in 384 AD and he petitioned for the restoration of the Altar of Victory.[63] In response, Ambrose, Bishop of Milan, wrote to the Emperor to pressure him to ignore the memorial of the Senate which Symmachus had sent. Ambrose had no qualms about addressing the Emperor plainly, "ponder well, I pray you, and examine the sect of the heathen, their utterances sound weighty and grand, but defend what is without capacity for truth. They speak of God and worship idols".[64] In the end the Altar of Victory was not replaced.

In Alexandria, in 391 AD, the Bishop wanted to convert the temple of Dionysus into a Church. He asked the Emperor Theodosius to hand over the temple to him and this was granted. This success led the Bishop to lay claim on all the temples in the city which he took control of, even parading their treasures through the main square. Pagans of the city responded by taking over the Serapeum and holding Christians captive there. The Bishop sought the Emperor's intervention and a letter was sent handing over all the temples to the Bishop.[65] In 407 AD, a further Imperial decree was issued from Rome stating,

> "If any images stand even now in the temples and shrines...they shall be torn from their foundations...The buildings themselves of the temples which are situated in cities or towns shall be vindicated to public use. Altars shall be destroyed in all places".[66]

In other words, within a century of Christians being persecuted, non-Christian practices were now being outlawed.

An Imperial edict issued in 423 AD declares,

> "We especially command those persons who are truly Christians or who are said to be, that they shall not abuse the authority of religion by laying violent hands on Jews and pagans who are living quietly and attempting nothing disorderly or contrary to law. For if such Christians should be violent against persons living in security or should plunder their goods,

they shall be compelled to restore not only that property that they took away, but after suit they shall also be compelled to restore triple or quadruple that amount that they robbed".[67]

The fact that this legislation was deemed necessary suggests that individual Christians and even official Church delegations were increasingly inclined to lay "violent hands on Jews and pagans". This edict suggests that by the early fifth century the Imperial administration was uncomfortable with the lengths to which some Christians were going against pagan institutions. It is difficult to assess which came first, the destruction of pagan institutions or the legislation which enabled it. Markus summarises the situation succinctly.

"Christianity had become conscious of its power to impose itself on Roman society. It had a sense of its mission to conquer the world for the gospel, and a confidence in its ability to do so very quickly. This sense of mission and confidence could release powerful passions and serve as a channel for the violence never far beneath the surface of late Roman urban life".[68]

There are plenty of examples of Church leaders initiating anti-pagan destruction under the auspices of state support and sometimes using monks to do the dirty work. In his *Oration* to the Emperor Theodosius, Libanius (c314-c394 AD) describes "black-garbed people" (by which he means monks) who,

"Run to the temples, bringing with them wood, and stones, and iron, and when they have not these, hands and feet...walls are pulled down, images are carried off and altars are overturned: the priests all the while must be silent upon pain of death. When they have destroyed one temple they run to another, and a third".[69]

These monks were going far beyond the law and seem to have had some measure of Church support. It would appear that Libanius' appeal to the Emperor fell on deaf ears because anti-pagan partnerships between Bishops and Emperors continued to develop.

Theodoret records how, soon after John Chrysostom's elevation as Bishop of Constantinople, he heard that pagan worship was still strong in Phoenicia. In response, "John got together certain monks who were filled with divine zeal, armed them with Imperial edicts and dispatched them against the idols' shrines".[70] In this case, the funding did not come from the Imperial treasury, but John "persuaded certain wealthy and faithful women to make liberal contributions, pointing out to them how great would be the blessing their generosity would win".[71] This contrasts with the more usual gentleness of John as, for example, when he waxes eloquent about the martyr St. Babylas, commending him as one who "bore off the most dangerous of our passions, anger".[72] One wonders if John came to regret the apparent anger which he directed toward the people of Phoenicia? Certainly, around the same time Ambrose displays some unease with the monks' methods admitting that "the monks commit many crimes".[73] Yet, on the other hand, Ambrose feels compelled to complain when he feels that "Timasius the General began to be over-vehement against the monks".[74]

Augustine also clearly felt that there was a place for force in the fight against paganism. In a sermon delivered at Carthage in June 401 AD, he reminded his listeners that the Romans had pulled down the idols in Rome before asking them why idols still stood in Carthage? He longed for his listeners to shout, "as in Rome so also in Carthage!"[75] Reading this it is hard not to agree with MacMullen that sermons like this were clear incitement to violent action, "for mobs must be worked up, the impulse spreads, and region and times alike were inflammable".[76]

Indeed, violence did ensue on occasion. In his letter to the magistrates of Suffectum, Augustine laments the fact that the people of the city killed 60 Christians. But this was in response to the Christians' destruction of a statue of Hercules.[77] By the mid-fifth century a Church Synod at Arles made it clear that it was a neglect of duty if any Bishop had not extinguished all worship of idols in his territory and penalties were decreed for any land owner who permitted idol worship on his estates.

Another century later, Caesarius the Bishop of Arles, until 542 AD, was clear that the forces of the State should be used to defeat paganism: "formerly the [State authorities] persecuted Christians for the sake of idols; now they persecute idols for the sake of Christ".[78] Kreider reminds us that in the second century Christianity grew largely through the evangelistic activities of ordinary people of "uninstructed and rustic character" before contrasting this to the situation in the sixth century.[79] "Four centuries later Caesarius, building on the tradition of Augustine, was now urging it to grow by top-down means, mobilising the influence and clout of local elites".[80] MacMullen summarises the situation memorably, "laws mattered less. They should be thought of as licences to take action, like a hunting licence today".[81]

In addition to anti-Pagan legislation and to Church authorities' use of that legislation to destroy pagan installations, a further 'method' developed in the form of direct force being applied to people to make them convert to Christianity. The account of the life of Porphyry the Bishop of Gaza (c347-420 AD), written by Mark the Deacon, gives a fascinating insight into the development of the idea that State force could be used to make Christians.

A delegation was sent from Gaza to request that Imperial edicts be issued instructing that the temples of Gaza be destroyed. The delegation met first with the Empress who was well disposed to them and when the Emperor came in she "told him the business of the Bishops, and asked him that the temples of Gaza might be destroyed".[82] However, the Emperor replied saying,

> *"I know that that city is idolatrous, but it is well disposed in the matter of the paying of taxes, contributing much money. If therefore we come suddenly upon them, and frighten them, they will flee and we shall lose so much tribute. But if it seems good, we shall afflict them piecemeal, taking away the dignities from the idol madmen and the other civic offices, and will command their temples to be shut up and give oracles no longer. For when they are afflicted and brought altogether into a strait place, they will acknowledge the truth. For a change that is over sudden is a heavy thing for subjects to bear".*[83]

Clearly the Emperor had no problem using his power to make people convert to Christianity, but he was also sufficiently politically aware to exercise caution in the execution of this power. This incident took place early in the fifth century but 100 years later the Emperor Justinian (527-565 AD) had no qualms at all about forcing pagans to convert to Christianity. He issued a decree (c531 AD) which ordered everyone in Athens who had not been baptised to assemble with their families in churches to receive instruction in Christian faith followed by baptism. Anyone who refused would be deprived of all their property, and if they were found to be sacrificing to idols, they would be executed.[84]

Later, the Emperor Tiberius (578-582 AD) ordered the local army commander at a town in Phoenicia called Baalbek-Heliopolis to move against the non-Christians in the community. As a result, the commander, Theopolius, "proceeded at once from Palestine to Heliopolis, and after arresting numerous heathens, recompensed them as their audacity deserved, humbling them and crucifying them, and slaying them with the sword".[85]

Towards the end of the fourth century another type of coercion to convert developed. This involved Church leaders urging landowners to erect churches on their estates and to bring their tenants to worship even if they had to be forced.[86] Salzman, in her study of how Italy was Christianised, concludes that this was the main means by which pagans living in rural areas were converted.[87] This conclusion is largely based on the sermons of Bishop Maximus of Turin (c380-c465 AD) which make clear that the *domini* (landlords) "had the duty to exercise control, because they would be held entirely responsible for idolatric practices on their estates".[88] The task was urgent and so Maximus urged his aristocratic listeners not to neglect "your people; for there is hardly one of you whose fields are not polluted by idols, hardly any estate held free from worship to demons".[89]

In the following century, Caesarius of Arles appealed to landlords to do all that was necessary to stamp out paganism.

> *"Chastise those who you know to be [guilty]; warn them very harshly; scold them very severely. And if they are not corrected, beat them if you have the power; and if they'll not improve by this, cut off their hair too. And if they still persevere, bind them in iron shackles, so that those whom the grace of Christ does not hold, a chain may hold".*[90]

Another century later Pope Gregory recommends to his Bishops in Sardinia that rent increases be used to push tenants towards conversion. "If any peasant should be found so perfidious and obstinate as to refuse to come to the Lord God, he must be weighted with so great a burden of payment as to be compelled by the very pain of the exaction to hasten to the right way".[91]

In this brief survey of anti-pagan legislation and other means of coercion used in an attempt to enforce Christian belief, the question must continually arise as to just how effective this was as a means of conversion. It is certainly true that temples are more easily closed than hearts changed. Even early in this new era of Church-State relations, Eusebius observed that when Constantine prohibited pagan books, "some, intimidated by the Emperor's threats, disguising their real sentiments, crept secretly into the Church".[92] Their conversion was far from real and it was not only Christian writers who observed this.

In his plea to the Emperor Theodosius against the destruction of pagan temples, Libanius, writing in 386 AD, said,

"By this means some have been converted, and brought to embrace the same religious sentiments with themselves. Do not be deceived by what they say; they only pretended, but are not convinced: for they are averse to nothing more than this, though they say the opposite. For the truth is, they have not changed the objects of their worship, but only appear to have done so. They join themselves with them in appearance, and outwardly perform the same things that they do: but when they are in a praying posture, they address to no-one, or else they invoke the gods".[93]

Legislative change and other methods of forcing people to Christianity may have brought people into the churches but were much less effective in bringing people to real faith in Christ.

PUBLIC WORSHIP

After the conversion of Constantine, liturgy became public. Services were no longer held in secret or closed to outsiders. Anyone was invited to attend. In tandem with this, liturgies became more elaborate and much grander in scale. One of the most obvious changes in the public worship of the Church was "the way the Church expanded its physical presence" by means of magnificent church buildings which began to appear.[94]

"Christian architecture, a phrase which would have almost seemed self-contradictory before the fourth century, shows most dramatically the impact of Constantine on Christianity".[95] Often wealthy aristocrats funded these buildings which became 'title-Churches' named after particular benefactors.[96]

In these new grand buildings the liturgy also became more elaborate. Congregations were no longer solely comprised of committed Christians and so, "in order to impress upon worshippers the holiness of participation in the body and blood of Christ, the Eucharistic liturgy became a good deal more formal and elaborate".[97] The congregation would stand in the 'court of the people,' which could be divided into up to seven naves in the largest churches.[98] One wonders what the impressions of these people were as they stood there. Certainly, it all must have seemed very grand, but also rather remote.

There is also some evidence that music and hymnology played a part in attracting people to the Christian faith. Augustine speaks of how he was deeply affected by the musical worship in Milan. "How greatly did I weep in my hymns and canticles, deeply moved by the voices of thy sweet-speaking Church! The voices flowed into my ears, and the truth was poured forth into my heart, whence the agitation of my piety overflowed, and my tears ran over, and blessed was I therein".[99]

Certainly, there was an increasing emphasis on the development of music in the churches of the fourth and fifth centuries. There would often be people to lead the singing and choirs became common.[100] Furthermore, "just as the catechetical teaching stressed the wholeness of the sacrifice that was offered in the Eucharist and the importance of approaching it with fear and trembling, so too the prayers, hymns and procedures that took place within the service were designed to instil awe and reverence".[101] In Antioch, Bishop Severus made use of hymns to draw people who were hanging around the public places of the town into his Church.[102]

It is significant that the grand churches, built during and after Constantine's reign, began to be referred to as 'temples' and 'sanctuaries'.[103] Additionally, the Church increasingly organised parades and other events in public places in the town again as a display of Christianity to those outside the Church.[104] However, Bradshaw helpfully summarises the tension inherent in all of this between,

> "On the one hand, the desire to make a clear distinction between pagan and Christian practices and ideas, and on the other hand, the desire to use the images and vocabulary of paganism to communicate to the world around the true meaning of Christianity as the fulfilment of everything to which other religions had dimly pointed".[105]

This tension continues to be apparent in the Church of today. It is always an open question as to how much of pagan culture to allow to influence the worship of the Church so as to attract pagans without compromising and diluting that worship to the point that it is less than Christian.

MISSION INSIDE THE CHURCH

Towards the end of a long sermon, Basil of Caesarea (330-379 AD) apologises to his congregation for detaining them so long before making it clear that his apology is somewhat half-hearted and that he believes they are much better sitting in church listening to him because he fears what they would be getting up to when they leave.

"If I dismiss this assembly, some will run to the dice, where they will find bad language, sad quarrels and the pangs of avarice. There stands the devil; enflaming the fury of the players with the dotted bones, transporting the same sums of money from one side of the table to the other...he who does not play spends his leisure elsewhere. What frivolities come from his mouth! What follies strike his ears? Leisure without the fear of the Lord is, for those who do not know the value of time, a school of vice".[106]

Basil then concludes with the hope that his words have been of help to them, "at least by occupying you here they have prevented you from sinning. Thus, the longer I keep you, the longer you are out of the way of evil".[107] We can imagine how the congregation felt about being addressed in this way, but it certainly gives some insight into the changed situation from the fourth century onwards. By then congregations were made up of people with varying levels of commitment. Presumably those who were really committed Christians still attended worship but so did many other people who were there for reasons of social convention or political advancement. Others were in attendance because they liked the music or appreciated the oratorical skills of the preacher.

In the earlier centuries Christians had a distinct identity. If someone converted to Christianity, it usually meant a clear break with their former life and it often meant that they were no longer in the mainstream of society. "Now Christian identity seemed to require less of a break with previous lifestyles and even religious practices than it once demanded".[108] By this time there was a clear need for mission to take place within the Church.

This was a new development. In previous centuries, congregations were made up of committed Christians who had been through a period of catechesis (teaching) leading up to their baptism before they were allowed to fully attend services. However, in these new circumstances, Bishops, catechists and other preachers had a huge role to play in drawing to the faith people who were already attending services. A study of their sermons reveals two main concerns which they addressed – preaching to convert those in the pews and challenging professing Christians to live out their faith.

In his *First Catechetical Instruction*, Augustine mentions "men who are drunkards, covetous, extortionists, gamblers, adulterers, fornicators, lovers of shows, wearers of idolatrous charms, soothsayers, astrologers, or diviners" before going on to point out that he sees "many who are called Christians given to these practices and doing them and championing and recommending and promoting the adoption of them".[109] So, clearly there were lots of professing Christians in the churches of Hippo who saw no contradiction in their continuing involvement with various forms of paganism.

Cyril of Jerusalem recognised that even catechumens who had been baptised and taken part in the Eucharist for the first time still may have had mixed motives. In his introductory lecture he addresses them,

> *"Possibly…you have come on another pretext. It is possible that a man is wishing to play court to a woman, and came here on that account. The remark applies in like manner to women also in their turn. A slave also perhaps wishes to please his master, and a friend his friend. I accept this bait for the hook, and welcome you, though you came with an evil purpose".*[110]

The congregations of the churches in the fourth century also contained many people who had become catechumens but had never gone on for baptism. Indeed, as exemplified by Constantine himself, it became increasingly common for people to delay their baptism until near death. As a result, there was a "large, amorphous group of unbaptised 'Christians' hesitating and temporising, deferring the time when they would be willing to submit themselves to the rigours of conversion".[111] Preachers of the fourth century urged them to fully commit themselves.

A century later the situation had changed again as evidenced by the sermons of Caesarius of Arles (468-542 AD). Caesarius drew extensively from Augustine's work in his own preaching, "but there was one striking difference between Augustine and Caesarius; whereas Augustine had appealed to as yet unbaptised catechumens to be converted, Caesarius urged conversion upon baptised Christians, even upon clerics".[112]

By now there were people who simply talked among themselves during the services and others even lay down, as evidenced by one of Caesarius' sermons where he preached,

> *"I exhort you with fatherly care that, whenever the lessons are read or the word of God is preached, no-one lie down on the ground, unless per chance, a very serious illness compels it. Even then no-one should lie down, but sit up and listen attentively with eager heart to the words that are preached".*[113]

Stephen the Deacon's biography of Caesarius tells us that as the Bishop "looked down from the altar after the reading of the Gospel, Caesarius saw some people leaving the church who particularly refused to listen to the Word, that is the sermon, of the blessed man".[114] As a result of this, Caesarius often gave orders for the doors to be locked after the reading of the Gospel so that people could not leave before the sermon.[115] He is well described as "an indefectible moral teacher, he persisted in his efforts to raise the tone of his church despite opposition and indifference to his plain speaking".[116]

Another generation later Martin of Braga (d579 AD) presented a sermon to one of the Bishops under him, Polemius, presumably intending it to be imitated by him and by other Bishops. Addressing those who were already baptised he declares, "You have abandoned the sign of the cross that you accepted at baptism, and pay heed instead to signs of the devil".[117] He goes on to urge them to "make an agreement with God in your heart, such that you will no more worship the devil, nor adore anything other than God in heaven, nor murder, nor commit adultery or fornication, nor steal, nor bear false witness".[118] Again it is clear that there was an ongoing need for mission *within* the Church.

THE ROLE OF THE BISHOP

The scope and complexity of the role of Bishops grew in ways that would have been unthinkable during the first three Christian centuries. Before Constantine, Bishops had little profile, position or respect in the wider society. Indeed, during times of persecution, they were sometimes the first to be martyred, probably in the hope that their death would demoralise and perhaps dissipate their congregations. However, in the centuries after Constantine their role and profile in society became at least as important as their functions in the Church.

During the fourth century the Bishop of a given town increasingly came to be seen as an important civic dignitary. This quickly led to involvement in matters far beyond the Church *per se*. We get an early insight into this through the letters of Basil, Bishop of Caesarea in the mid-fourth century, which indicate that he played a strategic role in the civic administration of Caesarea. For example, in one of his letters he mentions an Imperial levy, which he seems to be responsible for collecting.[119] It also appears that Basil was regularly involved in seeking to negotiate tax relief for various groups such as clergy, monks and even iron-workers.[120]

From Constantine onwards, Bishops were increasingly given official sanction to act as judges and arbiters in disputes. Again, this took increasing amounts of time as they sometimes had to listen to large numbers of cases. Their role as civic leaders became even more prominent in the fifth century when parts of the Western Empire in particular came under pressure from barbarian invaders.

It is difficult to determine whether or not the increased prestige and importance of Bishops to the social fabric of Roman cities became a 'method of mission' by increasing peoples' attraction to the Church. Certainly, it is easy to envisage that when society was breaking down due to barbarian influences, people would flee to the Church and gather under their Bishop simply in an attempt to derive some security as to their future.

Furthermore, in earlier times when Bishops were involved in petitioning Imperial officials on behalf of individuals, it no doubt led to much gratitude in the individuals who benefited as a result. On the other hand, if the Bishop acted in his judicial role in a way which the person in question disagreed with, then it seems likely that his or her view of Christ and the Church would be coloured forever.

In addition, the old adage that power corrupts certainly could apply. There is a story of Bishop Paulinus in the fifth century who wished for the view of his newly built martyrium (a church or shrine built over the tomb of a Christian martyr) to be improved by clearing a large open space in front of it. However, the owners of the homes and the workplace which were in the way were uncooperative. In the event all of their buildings were 'miraculously' burned down supposedly by the martyr Felix to whom the Bishop gave thanks as a result![121] It is not difficult to imagine what the people who lost their property in this way thought of the Bishop and his Church afterwards.

The social work of the Church has already been discussed but it should be noted that often the local Bishop was the lynch-pin for this work. It was he who oversaw the acquisition of funds and their distribution. Often this led to Bishops setting up large institutions and charities. Notable in this regard is Basil of Caesarea who founded hospices for the poor (for which he could usually gain tax exemption).[122]

The non-Christian Emperor Julian recognised how the Bishops played a large part in "giving coherence to the churches...he wanted [pagan] priests to provide a welfare agency for the destitute exactly as the churches had long done".[123] This coordinating role became even more important when parts of the Western Empire could be left in a political vacuum during the barbarian invasions. In that context, it was often the Bishops who ensured that food was properly distributed to the population.[124]

By the end of the sixth century, Venantius Fortunatus could write in his tribute to Bishop Carentius of Cologne, "you are food for the poor".[125] There is a certain tension apparent here in that, as Bishops became more and more pillars of society, then they would be less likely to prophetically critique the structural poverty in their society.

On the other hand, they had more resources with which to bring relief to the poor. As Davidson summarises,

> *"In terms of social action the practices of many Bishops were less radical in reality than their rhetoric suggested – they might roundly denounce such evils as abuse of the poor, the practice of usury or the ill-treatment of slaves, yet sometimes do little to seek to overturn the socio-economic structures upon which the injustices of the rich and powerful depended. Nevertheless, in a world in which the needs were truly enormous the work of alms-giving, care of the sick, and protection of the weak that was undertaken by the churches was considerable".*[126]

This social care must have had an impact in attracting people to the Church and to Christian faith and there is no doubt that the Bishops played a crucial role in ensuring that social care happened.

MISSIONARY EVANGELISTS

It might be expected that, after Constantine, there would be a resurgence in missionary evangelists given they could now preach in freedom without any risk of interference from the State and there would have been little need for fear about gathering a crowd of listeners together in a public place. In light of this, it seems surprising that, in fact, this did not again become a major method of mission in the fourth, fifth and sixth centuries. Having said that, it was not absent and some examples can be cited such as Philastrius who "travelled nearly over the whole Roman world preaching against pagans, Jews and heretics". [127]

Another example is Abraames who went to live in a pagan village on Mount Libanus where he "narrowly escaped death" at the hands of the inhabitants.[128] In due course, tax collectors moved into the village and those who couldn't pay were threatened with prison, but Abraames was able to raise a loan with which the tax arrears were cleared. Consequently, "by this charity he gained them all for Christ" and remained for three more years instructing them in Christian things before leaving them in the care of a priest.[129] Abraames then moved on to another location, "where he worked with the same cunning and enthusiasm".[130]

There were Bishops who either directly engaged in missionary activity themselves or sponsored others to do so in the less evangelised parts of their diocese and beyond. One of the best known examples is Martin of Tours (316-397 AD). "Apart from a minimum of episcopal administration Martin devoted…15 years to a concentrated mission among the peasant populations in the Loire and Seine Valleys where the deities of Romano-Celtic paganism held sway".[131]

In Northern Italy there is some evidence that Ambrose of Milan sought to create new Bishoprics in pagan dominated areas and appoint Bishops to them. "Imola at the beginning of his episcopate, Vercelli and Novara near the end of his life, were communities which benefited from his zeal".[132]

It is apparent, then, that most pioneer missionary work was executed by Bishops and other clergy. There is less evidence of independent pioneer missionaries. This is a natural consequence of the fact that in these centuries the Church was increasingly becoming an organised institution rather than a loose network of local groups and, in conjunction with this, the Church was becoming clergy dominated.

The examples mentioned above seem to be the exception rather than the rule and Wood is correct that "the history of the Christianisation of the Roman Empire is not one dominated by missionaries".[133] Yet, is this really surprising? During the fourth and fifth centuries many people came to the churches for all kinds of reasons and this fact was bound to lessen the missionary zeal of potential evangelists.

Indeed, the main struggle during this era was to call to faith those who came to church for social or other reasons and to deepen faith in those who had only nominally become Christians. In this context, further outreach to non-evangelised areas often took a back seat. At least that was the case within the Empire, but beyond its boundaries, where Christianity was not the State religion, things were different as we shall see in the next chapter.

CONCLUSION

The change in the fortunes of the Church in the centuries after the conversion of Constantine was remarkable in scope. It is hard to imagine a more radical difference in context between that in which the Church found itself at the beginning of the third century compared with the end of the fourth century. As a result, even though the essential message of Christianity had not changed, the means by which the Church grew was radically altered. The two main methods of 'mission' of the Church were now "inducement and compulsion".[134] State and Church became more and more allied and to become a Christian increasingly meant to enter the mainstream of society. The Church was no longer a relatively small but intensely committed band of people; now there was a large range of commitment within the Church. There were still those who were passionate about their faith, but, at the other end of the spectrum, there were many people in the pews who had at most a nodding acquaintance with Christ.

4

Mission Beyond the Mainstream of Roman Society

INTRODUCTION
During the centuries after the conversion of Constantine, the Christian Church moved from being a small, marginalised and sometimes persecuted minority to being at the centre of Roman society. No longer was it countercultural to be a Christian. This meant that Christian values and the values of the wider society progressively merged, while Christian leaders became powerful and influential figures in the Roman Empire. However, not all Christians were within the mainstream of Roman society.

Firstly, there were those who still lived within the political boundaries of the Roman Empire but tried to separate themselves from general society by withdrawing, often into remote locations. Secondly, there were Christians who lived or travelled beyond the political boundaries of the Roman Empire. This chapter will examine both of these groups.

MONASTICISM
A major feature of the development of Christianity is the emergence of monasticism. It is difficult to trace the exact source of this development, but it grew out of a tendency towards asceticism amongst some. The main impetus for this was the ending of the threat of persecution of Christians by the Imperial authorities. The motivation of many monks was "the spiritual imitation of martyrdom".[1] Another probable contributing factor is that the quickly increasing tax burden on small landholders drove some to

simply abandon their farms and flee to the wilderness, "flight from the world…included flight from the tax collector".[2]

The key principle of monasticism was withdrawal. Its followers came out of normal society either to be alone or to live in isolated communities in the desert, the mountains or even small islands (such as Skellig Michael in Co Kerry). The focus was on developing their own personal interaction with God in a setting isolated from the rest of society.

They did it because they thought it would make them better Christians. Their first concern was not the Church, but rather, their own personal pilgrimage. But our question here is, did this movement cause conversions to Christianity even though mission/evangelism was not the initial raison d'être of the ascetic/monastic movement?

Norris is correct that, "Monasticism in its numerous forms shaped countless Christian lives, either directly when people became monks or nuns or indirectly as secular Christians sought their advice".[3] If something leads to Christians becoming stronger then surely that strengthens the Church? On the other hand, it was, almost by definition, the most ardent and committed Christians who withdrew from society and the Church in this way, making it difficult to disagree with Chadwick that "their withdrawal unquestionably weakened the ordinary congregations".[4]

One notable development, largely in Syria, was the stylites – people who removed themselves from everyone by living on top of a column or pillar, which could be 20m tall. The best known of these was Simeon (c385-459 AD). Many people came to see him and some criticised his behaviour. But records also suggest that many believers were enthused and impressed by him and also that a number of pagans were converted through him.[5]

On the other hand, it is easy to imagine that some of the more extreme forms of asceticism which were practised would lead pagans to reject Christianity as sheer madness. There were some men who weighed themselves down with chains, others who went barefoot during winter and some women who wore male clothing and tried to grow beards. There were even some Christians who wore children's clothing on the basis that Jesus said, "unless you change and become like little children, you will never enter the kingdom of heaven".[6]

In some areas, monastic communities were established which were located reasonably close to towns and villages with which they maintained relations. *The Historia Monachorum* records that in Egypt, "some of them live in towns, some in the country, the best of them scattered through the desert".[7] Notably, Pachomius (c292-346 AD) tended to build his monasteries on the edge of a village and so,

> "Placed Egyptian ascetics on the border between the realm of the living and the abode of the dead. Some ventured far into the desert seeking a more absolute solitude, but most did not: the desert lay at hand when needed, as did the village. Ascetics supported themselves by handicrafts or by working as seasonal labourers, depending on others to buy their services and to sell them food and other necessities".[8]

The Historia Monachorum records a journey, which some Palestinian monks took amongst the monastic settlements that were developing in Egypt towards the end of the fourth century. On arrival at Nitra, which is said to be the most famous monastic settlement, they describe 50 dwellings gathered under a single Father, some with just one occupant and others living communally.[9] The travellers recorded that they were particularly struck by the warmth of the welcome they received because on their arrival, the monks rushed out of their cells offering bread and water and insisting on washing the travellers' feet. So, the writer concludes,

> "What can I say about their humanity, their work, their charity, since all of them beckoned us towards their own selves, not only fulfilling the obligation of hospitality, but also showing us the humility and gentleness and other virtues of this sort which are only learned by people thus separated from the world...Nowhere else had we seen such charity flourishing, nowhere such acts of compassion and eager hospitality".[10]

As monastic communities developed, hospitality given to visiting strangers became more organised. In his description of the monastery at Nitria, Palladius (b457/461 AD) wrote, "Next to the church is a guesthouse, where they receive the stranger who has arrived, until he goes away of his own accord, without limit of time, even if he remains two or three years".[11] It is likely that if someone enjoyed free hospitality in such a committed Christian community for a period of years it would surely greatly strengthen their faith if they were already converted or could well lead to their conversion if they were not already Christian.

A generation later Benedict (480-547 AD) told his followers,

> "Let all guests who arrive be received as Christ...In the greeting let all humility be shown to the guests, whether coming or going; with the head bowed down or the whole body prostrate on the ground, let Christ be adored in them as He is also received...Let the greatest care be taken, especially in the reception of the poor and travellers, because Christ is received more specially in them".[12]

Again, if a non-Christian were received in this manner it would be deeply impressive and may even lead them towards Christ.

As monastic communities developed, they increasingly engaged in social outreach. In the *Rules of Basil*, written for the monastery that he founded about 356 AD, we read, "it is God's will that we should nourish the hungry, give the thirsty to drink, clothe the naked".[13] Also, Palladius, in his *Lausiac History*, describes the large monasteries in Egypt which grew up around Pachomius. He describes one of these which had 300 monks and where he "found 15 tailors, seven smiths, four carpenters, 12 camel-drivers, and 15 fullers".[14] These were "economic units", but significant social outreach was a by-product as Palladius notes: "with their surplus output they provide for the needs of both the women's convents and the prisons".[15] They also kept pigs from which the meat was sold, "but the tit-bits are to be devoted to the sick and aged, because the neighbourhood is poor and populous".[16]

John Cassian (d363 AD) described how the monks in Egypt worked hard so as to, "collect an enormous store of provisions and food, and distribute it in the parts of Libya which suffer from famine and barrenness, and also in the cities, to those who are pining away in the squalor of prison".[17] As this level of social outreach work developed it must surely have impressed non-Christians. Rubenson summarises, "The strong emphasis on hospitality and care for the poor and sick resulted in making the monasteries of the fifth and sixth centuries into centres visited by all levels of society".[18]

However, by this time there was less and less need for people to go out into the wilderness to visit monasteries if they wanted to benefit from the monks' social outreach work.

> "Monks were becoming part of the daily experience of the great many town-dwellers in fifth and sixth century Gaul. Monks were present in towns and in their close neighbourhood, and could influence – just by being there? By example? Monastic practices were becoming familiar in ever widening circles".[19]

Indeed, it seems that this movement of monks back into the towns even began before the fifth century. In 390 AD, the Emperor Theodosius I instituted a law ordering all monks to stay in deserted places. However, two years later he had to cancel the law because "the monks had made themselves indispensable for civic administration by becoming providers of welfare for a growing poor and potentially disruptive layer of society".[20]

Sozomen offers some evidence that the lifestyle of monks strengthened the case for Christianity. In his *Ecclesiastical History*, he speaks of two heresies which were threatening to affect Christians in the region of Cilicia before concluding, "That these dogmas did not prevail and make further advance is to be attributed, in addition to the causes mentioned, especially to the monks of that period".[21] The reason for this, according to Sozomen, is that, "the people admired the monks who manifested their virtue by works and believed that they held right opinions".[22]

A further way in which solitary ascetics could influence ordinary people was when they offered advice. Such advice was greatly sought after and trusted because people felt that those who lived close to God were more likely to speak with divine inspiration. In the case of Anthony, the pressure of people seeking his advice forced him to move into a more remote location – his "Inner Mountain".[23]

Frend also observes that monks could be engaged to act as arbiters in disputes. For example, he notes that Simon Stylites, from his pillar, "maintained a lively contact with officials, forwarding petitions to them, acting as a court of appeal in cases over disputed weights and measures and unjust judicial decisions".[24] In this way, monks could offer justice and fairness which could be in short supply as well as, perhaps, providing a voice to the voiceless. Such a role of service could conceivably influence its recipients towards Christ.

In all of this it is difficult to assess how much the development of monasticism really did act as a 'method of mission' in that people were influenced towards Christianity. However, what is clearer is that as Christians left the churches which were mostly urban based and went out into the countryside, it did facilitate the spread of the Christian message in these rural areas. Monasteries sometimes "acted as staging grounds for those who tried to evangelise the surrounding areas".[25]

Foakes-Jackson points out that,

"We are apt to forget, whilst studying the often barren and profitless controversies of the age, the astonishing vitality of the Church in every

part of the world. If missionary zeal is a proof of life, the Christian Church was never more alive than at the close of our period. By AD 461 there were strong and vigorous Churches in Armenia, Iberia, Mesopotamia, Persia and Ethiopia. The gospel was preached in Sahara [while]...Ireland, which had never been incorporated in the Empire, was a province of the Roman Church; and Christianity had overstepped the wall of Hadrian, which the Romans had such difficulty in defending. Britain was overrun by heathen invaders who were powerless to eradicate what must have appeared to be but a feeble branch of the Christian Church. By means unknown to us, by missionaries whose names will never be revealed, every invader of Gaul and Italy, Spain and Africa, had heard of Christ".[26]

So, let us consider those who took the Christian message beyond the borders of the Roman Empire, whether as 'professional' missionaries or as ordinary Christian people who travelled to other places.

'PROFESSIONAL' MISSIONARIES

The detail of how Christianity first took root amongst Syriac-speaking people is uncertain but by "the fourth and fifth centuries, Syriac-speaking Christians were in the majority throughout the Roman diocese of the Orient. They also existed in great numbers in Mesopotamia".[27] In other words, Syriac Christians lived on both sides of the eastern border of the Roman Empire. This border was constantly changing and with it the fortunes of the Christians. If they were in the Roman Empire, then they benefited from being part of the official religion. On the other hand, if they ended up within the boundaries of the Persian Empire they had no such privilege and indeed, at times, were persecuted because they were perceived as having Roman sympathies.[28] However, one of the distinguishing features of Syriac Christianity was a definite missionary consciousness.

The *Odes of Solomon* contain some of the early writings of these Christians, although their dating is uncertain. We see the gospel depicted as a stream that,

"became a river great and broad; indeed it carried away everything...and the barriers which were built by men were not able to restrain it...for it spread over the surface of all the earth, and it filled everything. Then all the thirsty upon the earth drank, and thirst was relieved and quenched".[29]

This suggests a clear understanding of Christians' duty to spread the Good News. Meyendorff concurs, adding that "the missionary activity of Syrian Christians, frequently monks, also included travelling to foreign countries for the sake of the gospel".[30]

This foreign travel even extended as far as China. In 635 AD a monk known as Alopen arrived in the city of Ch'Ang-An, the capital city of the T'ang Dynasty.[31] He was well-received, with a senior member of the government being sent to meet him. Alopen was then officially escorted to the Emperor's palace where he was authorised to translate into Chinese the texts that he had brought with him. The resources of the large Imperial library were made available to him for this task. We are not told what the texts in question were and whether or not they included the Scriptures. However, the Emperor was impressed with what he read concluding, "If we carefully examine the meaning of the teaching it is mysterious, wonderful, full of repose…it is the salvation of living beings, it is the wealth of men. It is right that it should have free course under the sky".[32] Furthermore, the Emperor resourced the building of a monastery within the capital to which 21 ordained priests were attached. The inscription goes on to say that Alopen founded Christian monasteries in every prefecture.

The Christian message was also carried north. By far the most well known of the missionaries to the Goths (Germanic people originating in what is now northern Poland) was Ulfilas who led a substantial group of Christian refugees across the Danube where they were warmly received and allowed to settle on Roman soil. He spent the rest of his life at Nicopolis (a city on the southern shore of the Danube in what is now Bulgaria) caring for his congregations as well as studying, teaching and translating the Bible.[33] Ulfilas was more than a chaplain to those who had already become Christians. He was an evangelist and the Church grew under his episcopacy. However, regretfully from the point of view of this study, we know virtually nothing about his methods of mission, with one notable exception.

Philostorgius, Socrates and Sozomen all agree that Ulfilas committed the Gothic language to written form and then translated most of the Bible.[34] This must also have entailed educating the people in basic literacy. Sozomen summarises that Ulfilas "taught them the use of letters, and translated the Sacred Scriptures into their own language".[35] It seems most likely that this greatly facilitated the spread of Christianity. For Christian teaching to really take hold amongst a people they must have the Scriptures in their own language.

No doubt there were other missionaries in this area, but little is known of them. One other whose name we know is Eutyches. He is mentioned in the Letter of Basil (c329-379 AD), *To Ascholius* thanking him for the gift of some relics of Gothic martyrs that he had given to his church in Cappadocia. As we saw in Chapter Three, this letter laments the unholy lifestyle of Christians in Basil's diocese. He goes on to contrast the life of the missionary Eutyches and his like with the comfortable condition of Christians living in the Empire.

> *"You tell me of struggles of athletes, bodies lacerated for the truth's sake, savage fury despised by men of fearless heart, various tortures of persecutors, and constancy of the wrestlers through them all, the block and the water whereby the martyrs died. And what is our condition? Love is grown cold; the teaching of the Fathers is being laid waste; everywhere is shipwreck of the Faith".*[36]

This letter is placed towards the end of Basil's episcope and so describes the scene in the 370s AD. It is clear that Basil's understanding of mission at the frontiers is different to the mission of the Church within the Empire.

Of course, the message also came north-west, even to Ireland. Palladius stands as the first known figure in the history of Irish Christianity but we know little about him. He was soon to be followed by Patrick. The general shape of Patrick's life is well known but the details are vigorously debated and so many later legends were written about Patrick that it is easy to become confused.[37] However, we are fortunate in that there are two texts which are almost universally accepted as being written by Patrick himself – his *Confession* and his *Letter to Coroticus*.

In his *Confession*, he is adamant that the aim of his return to Ireland was to share Christianity, "I testify in truthfulness and gladness of heart before God and his holy angels that I never had any reason, except the gospel and his promises, ever to have returned to that nation from which I had previously escaped with difficulty".[38] Patrick's call is clearly focused:

> *"One should, in fact, fish well and diligently, just as the Lord foretells and teaches, saying, 'Follow me, and I will make you fishers of men...So it behoved us to spread our nets, that a vast multitude and throng might be caught for God...Just as the Lord says in the Gospel, admonishing and instructing: 'Go therefore and make disciples of all nations, baptising them in the name of the Father and of the Son and of the Holy Spirit,*

teaching them to observe all that I have commanded you; and lo, I am with you always to the end of time'".[39]

So, Patrick clearly understands the words of Jesus (which we call the Great Commission) as being urgently applicable to him. While the conviction that the gospel is for all the world is commonplace in the Church today, this was not so in Patrick's time. In fact, Patrick is the first person in recorded history to quote this text and take it literally.[40]

Patrick was utterly committed to this task. In his *Confession*, he tells of how he went against the will of his parents and resisted all their protests "that I might come to the Irish people to preach the gospel…and if I should be worthy, I am ready [to give] even my life without hesitation; and most willingly for His name".[41] So his undivided aim was to convert people to Christianity.

He was highly motivated and there is no doubt that many people became Christians as a result of his work, but what was his method of mission? Again, there is a frustrating scarcity of information available to us. As Thompson laments,

"Nothing could give more pleasure to the student of St. Patrick than a description of what happened when he entered for the first time a pagan, or almost wholly pagan, Irish village. What sort of person did he first seek out? What kind of thing did he say to them? How did he set about expounding the new religion and undermining their faith in the gods which had satisfied them and their ancestors hither to? The answers to these and countless similar questions are utterly beyond us".[42]

It is indeed frustrating that in the *Confession* and the *Letter to Coroticus* Patrick makes little or no attempt to describe his methods. Presumably this is because, in these documents, he was addressing people who already knew how he operated, because that is what had prompted them to criticise his methods.

Nevertheless, from Patrick's own writings we can glean several hints. Firstly, we know that when Patrick entered a new area he went first to the local political leaders attempting to win their favour before continuing. As he writes in his *Confession*: "you know from experience how much I was paying to those who were administering justice in all the regions, which I visited often"[43] and also, "From time to time I gave rewards to the kings".[44] It seems that he had some success in this because he claims that "the sons of the Irish and the daughters of the chieftains are to be seen as monks and virgins of Christ".[45] Hinson is probably correct in that approaching the Irish tribal chieftains directly was "perhaps...the only reasonable entrée in view of tribal solidarity".[46] The people in Irish society, at that time, were clearly identified into strict classes – kings, noblemen, craftsmen and *brehons* (judges), freed men and slaves so that Christian clergymen such as Patrick would not fit into this scheme and, therefore, such people "would be outcasts...unable to call with confidence upon the protection of the law".[47]

In this context, then, he would need the permission of the local hierarchy wherever he went, especially if he travelled "as far as the outermost regions beyond which no one lived, and where no one had ever penetrated before, to baptise or to ordain clergy or to confirm people".[48]

One other feature of Patrick's method is that he did not operate alone. In his *Confession* he mentions others "who travel with me".[49]

Hunter, while recognising the difficulty due to lack of reliable resources, attempts to piece together a more detailed outline of the typical modus operandi of Patrick's mission team. He suggests that, after convincing the local leaders in a new settlement to convert or at least allow them to stay, Patrick and his followers would set up a camp near where the people lived. They would then share in conversation and ministry including praying for the sick and the possessed, whilst also offering counsel to people and mediating in conflicts. They would also engage in some open air speaking usually including parable, story, song and perhaps visual symbols.[50]

This all sounds plausible, but the difficulty is that most of it is based on Muirchu's *Life of St. Patrick* and Tirechan's unnamed, seventh-century collection of stories about Patrick's mission, both of which are historically unreliable. However, we can be confident that Patrick would have understood the language and customs of his listeners given that he had lived for six years in Ireland as a slave. Davidson argues convincingly that,

> *"It is apparent that Patrick did make some real efforts to enculturate his gospel in the patterns, practices, and values of ancient Irish life. Though he was sharply critical of many aspects of ancient Celtic religion, he also had an understanding of the spiritual traditions of those to whom he preached, and he was prepared to appeal to elements of their pagan past in order to earth his evangel in symbols and ideals with which his hearers could identify."*[51]

Patrick outlines his motivation for preaching the gospel before continuing, "I am sending forth many fishers and hunters, says the Lord".[52] Dana Robert picks up on Patrick's use of the word "hunters" noting that, whilst the Bible talks about fishermen it never mentions hunters. Patrick's adoption of this word "gives a tantalising hint of the way he must have adapted the Biblical stories to the circumstances of the Celtic warrior/hunter's culture in which he lived".[53]

Patrick and his helpers certainly faced opposition. While most stories about his miraculous confrontations with the druids are almost certainly apocryphal, there is little reason to doubt that leaders of the long-standing traditional Irish religions would have opposed what Patrick was trying to do. Patrick did not shrink back from contradicting what he understood to be mistaken beliefs amongst his pagan listeners. For example, Ó hÓgáin points out that Patrick "obviously regarded solar religion as a particularly powerful pagan phenomenon".[54] So, in his *Confession*, Patrick clearly attempts to make the sun subordinate to Christ.[55]

In addition to religious leaders, some of the kings and tribal leaders whom Patrick attempted to convert would have harshly rejected his advances. The *Letter to Coroticus* highlights the fact that Patrick's converts could be in danger from hostile military forces. Nevertheless, "he outlived his enemies and wore down the opposition; at the time of his death Ireland was a largely Christian country".[56] So, while we still know little about his methods, it is evident that Patrick's mission was a success and he left behind a securely established Christian Church in Ireland.

Another Irish itinerant figure of note is Columba (c521-597 AD) who was born in Co. Donegal but departed Ireland, landing on the island of Iona off the west coast of Scotland where he founded a monastery.[57] Bede claims that within two years Columba had begun missionary work on mainland Scotland (or Alba as it was then known) where the people were known as 'Picts'. "In the year of our Lord 565…there came into Britain from Ireland a famous priest and abbot, marked as a monk by habit and manner of life, whose name was Columba, to preach the word of God to the provinces of the northern Picts".[58]

Despite Bede's claim, there is some doubt as to whether mission was really Columba's motive for sailing to Scotland. Adomnan describes Columba as leaving Ireland because he was "choosing to be a pilgrim for Christ".[59] There are many examples of this Celtic monastic tendency. To leave the familiarity and security of home and to travel into the unknown was seen as a way of advancing one's spiritual life.[60] However, very often "pilgrimage merged insensibly into mission".[61] Columba's reason for leaving Ireland may have been as an exile or political refugee, or it could have been to foster political alliances to preserve the Dalriadan settlement in Scotland. It is likely that his motive was a combination of factors, but, as Frend puts it, "Columba's aim was no doubt partly missionary".[62]

The poem *Amrae Coluimb Chille* composed soon after Columba's death claims that he preached to the "tribes of Tay" who lived on the eastern coast of Scotland.[63] To get there from Iona, Columba would have crossed the whole country. Adomnan also records that on two occasions Columba travelled as far as the stronghold of King Bridei, which was near Inverness in north-eastern Scotland. Adomnan's biography of Columba is laced with improbable miracle stories, but it does offer some clear evidence that, as Fletcher puts it, "Columba the monastic founder was also, on occasion, an evangelist".[64]

Adomnan tells of one occasion when Columba was travelling through central Scotland. Approaching Loch Ness, he felt the Holy Spirit telling him to make haste to meet an elderly man who needed to hear the gospel of Jesus Christ. As a result, Columba hurried on until he reached Glen Urquhart. "There he found an old man called Emchath, who heard and believed the Word of God preached to him by the saint and was baptised".[65]

Columba did some evangelistic preaching while travelling, but the main method he employed was the establishment of monasteries. Fletcher summarises:

> *"The monasteries that were founded by the exiled holy men had something of the character of mission stations. It was not that they were established primarily among pagans; indeed, they could not have been, dependent as they were on wealthy patrons, necessarily Christian (if we except the case of the pagan would-be benefactors in Ireland), for their endowments. Columba settled among the Christian Irish of Dalriada, Columbanus in the Christian kingdom of the Francs. But their monastic communities were situated on the margins of Christendom and had what might be called 'diffusive potential' among nearby laity who were Christian only in the most nominal of senses".*[66]

A later product of the monastic community which Columba established at Iona was Aidan who was sent to the land of Northumbria (present day north-east England and south-east Scotland) when Oswald became the king there in 633 AD. Soon after his accession to the throne, Oswald, who had spent time in exile in Iona, sent a request that they send a "bishop of the Scots to administer the word of faith to him and his nation".[67] Iona quickly responded but the first Bishop dispatched had an unsuccessful ministry; he was a rather austere man who made severe demands on his pagan listeners. When Aidan heard this he responded,

> *"You were more severe to your unlearned hearers than you ought to have been and did not at first, conforming to the Apostolic rule, give them the milk of more easy doctrine, till being by degrees nourished by the Word of God, they should be capable of greater perfection, and be able to practice God's sublimer precepts".*[68]

As a result, Aidan himself was sent to Northumbria and Bede records that,

> *"He traversed both town and country on foot, never on horseback, unless compelled by some urgent necessity; to that end that, as he went, he might turn aside to anyone he saw, either rich or poor, and call upon them, if infidels, to receive the mystery of the faith or if they were believers, to strengthen them in the faith, and to stir them up by words and actions to giving of alms and the performance of good works".*[69]

Aidan's tendency to walk meant that he was more likely to make personal contact with people. Horse riding would set him above people and portray an image of wealth and power. Certainly, his mission was more effective because he met people at eye level.[70] Aidan was not very proficient in the English language, especially early in his ministry. However, King Oswald was fluent in the Irish tongue, having lived on Iona. Consequently, Bede paints the following remarkable picture,

> *"The king also humbly and willingly in all cases giving ear to his admonitions, industriously applied himself to build and extend the Church of Christ in his kingdom; so that, when the bishop, who was not skilful in the English tongue, preached the gospel, it was most delightful to see the king himself interpreting the Word of God to his commanders and ministers, for he had perfectly learned the language of the Scots during his long banishment".*[71]

This combination of an eloquent preacher whose words were being interpreted by the king himself must have made for a powerful and effective presentation of the gospel to the Northumbrian peoples.

Aidan also attempted to show the love of God by example. Any gifts which he received, he immediately distributed to the poor or used them to ransom those who had been sold as slaves.[72] He also had an eye to the future and made a point of taking some of his converts under his wing for further instruction to develop an indigenous Northumbrian priesthood.

It would be wrong to give the impression that the mission work in Northumbria was just an individual enterprise by Aidan. Bede records that "many came daily into Britain from the country of the Scots, and with great devotion preached the Word to those provinces of the English, over which King Oswald reigned, and those among them that had received priest's orders administered the grace of Baptism to the believers".[73]

The Irish monks and their English trainees still tended to live in community. Early on, Aidan established a monastery on the island of Lindisfarne and, as the work spread, more monasteries with associated churches and schools were built. These would have had an impact on the community. Irish monasteries in a pagan environment would have stood out and offered people hope for a better way of living. The mission of Columbanus (also known as Columban) provides further evidence of this.

Columbanus (c550-615 AD) received his formation at St. Comgall's monastery in Bangor, Co. Down. Then, around 585 AD, he took 12 companions and travelled to Gaul (France). He settled in Burgundy and founded three monasteries in close proximity to each other (Luxeuil, Anegray and Fontaine). They were all chosen because they were located in isolated, desolate countryside. The Rule in these monasteries was very strict and complete obedience was expected. Food was minimal, work was tough and punishments were severe. Nevertheless, the communities prospered for two decades until Queen Brunhilde was greatly angered by Columbanus and forced him to go to Nantes with a view to sailing home. However, in the end he travelled up the Rhine to Switzerland stopping on the shores of Lake Constance. One of his followers, Gall, founded an abbey there, but Columbanus travelled on across the Alps into Northern Italy to establish another centre at Bobbio.[74]

Our main interest is the methods Columbanus used, but there is ongoing debate as to whether Columbanus himself had any real interest in mission. Essentially he was, "a *Peregrinus Pro Christo*, that is, a man who abandoned his homeland in order to follow the Gospel injunction of abandoning for

Christ's sake the society in which he had been brought up".[75] His primary aim, like the monks of Syria and Egypt, was to deepen his own walk with Christ.

His secondary purpose was to encourage others into monastic life. Columbanus' main biographer, Jonas, tells us that, when Columbanus finally agreed to be deported from his monastery at Luxeuil, he comforted his brethren, who were upset, by telling them to put their trust in God and assuring them that "this was not an injury to him or his followers, but an opportunity to increase the number of monks".[76]

On the other hand, Columbanus always aimed to choose remote, inhospitable areas to build his monasteries, which invariably meant there were few people living around; someone with a primarily missionary heart would have wanted to remain near large populations.

Nevertheless, Jonas does show us hints of missionary intent, "Once Columban thought of going to the land of the Wends, who are also called Slavs, in order to illuminate their darkened minds with the light of the gospel and to open the way of truth to those who had always wandered in error".[77] Nonetheless, Dunn is largely correct that, "Columbanus' activities were those of a conscientious monastic *peregrinus* who had removed himself from his homeland and centres of Christian cult, only to feel obliged to preach to those whom he encountered on his way".[78] However, although preaching the gospel and spreading the faith was not Columbanus' main motivation, the faith was spread as a result of his travels.

On meeting the Frankish King Theudebert, Jonas records Columbanus as promising him that, if he had his support, "he would gladly remain there longer and try to sow the seeds of faith in the hearts of the neighbouring peoples".[79] A location was agreed to which Columbanus sailed up the Rhine. "At length they arrived at the place designated, which did not wholly please Columban; but he decided to remain, in order to *spread the faith* among the people, who were Swabians".[80]

Jonas tells us that, when they first arrived in Brittany, Columbanus and his companions spent some time recovering their strength and making plans before deciding to enter Gaul because, "they wanted zealously and shrewdly to enquire into the disposition of the inhabitants in order to remain longer if they found they could sow the seeds of salvation; or in case they found the hearts of the people in darkness, go on to the nearest nations".[81] This surely portrays a missionary intent. Indeed, Jonas summarises "everywhere that he went the noble man preached the gospel".[82] So, was Columbanus a monk or a missionary? Fletcher responds that, "The antithesis is misplaced. To be the kind of monk he was, in the age in which he lived, was also to be an evangelist".[83]

Whatever the effect of his preaching, the biggest impact Columbanus made for the gospel was through the establishment of his monasteries. Hinson, who argues that within the Roman Empire, Christianity spread through the planting of churches, goes on to contend that "in the Barbarian mission, monasteries served a function very similar to that filled earlier by the churches".[84] Shelley summarises that the monasteries established through Columbanus "became centres of evangelisation".[85] Jonas tells us that when the monastery at Luxeuil was established, "people streamed in from all directions in order to consecrate themselves to the practice of religion".[86]

How and why did this happen? An understanding of the situation in Gaul helps to answer to that question. For the local residents, "the white-robed monks seemed to have come, not from a different country but from a different world".[87] Since the conversion of Clovis a century earlier, France was at least nominally Christian, but Frankish chieftains sought to emulate Roman Emperors on a smaller scale. However, unlike Roman Emperors, they never had enough cash to keep their troops happy or to pay off underlings on whom their power depended. Instead, they paid with land which meant that their own territories dwindled whilst underling estates increased. The only thing the King could do was capture more land, "but after a hundred years the captured lands, passing from hand to hand, were divided, badly farmed, exhausted and of little value. There was a general running down of the state".[88]

Coupled with this was a religious decline, Bishops became more like secular rulers and the message of Christianity was heard and seen less. Also, since the break-up of the Western Empire, international commerce had declined and raw materials had to be found locally rather than through export and import. This resulted in townspeople moving out to the countryside where Christianity never had strong roots. "With this rural trend the Church's influence sank even lower".[89] Jonas concludes that by the time Columbanus arrived "the Christian faith had almost departed from that country".[90]

The only exception to this was some of the French monasteries which in earlier days had played a part in taking Christianity to Ireland. However, in some of these asceticism had gone to extreme lengths. So, "between the self-persecution of the paranoid, and the licence of the buccaneer, there seemed no middle path".[91]

As Lehane describes,

"Among all this, whatever the locals thought of the immigrant Irish men, they must certainly have been impressed. Into an atmosphere of shift and deception walked bands of Irish with a clear and unequivocal sense of purpose. That purpose had nothing whatever to do with vendettas or luxury or making money or winning territories; little with emaciating themselves into scrawny and impotent worshippers of a far-removed god. Worship came first, but good worship presupposed good health. They revived long-term farming methods on the land they took over. With the product they fed themselves, gave free provisions to the needy, and sold the rest for money to expand their activities. They were healthy in mind as much as body and gave no precedence to material things. They showed how to order things for the best in circumstances which were far from good".[92]

The Suevians who lived around Columbanus' three monasteries at Annegray, Luxeuil and Fontaines depended mostly on subsistence agriculture. To them the idea of a peace-loving God, with a Son who gave himself up to execution would have been incomprehensible. But, in this context, Christian witness primarily through actions proved effective.

"As time passed other things than doctrine began to modify Suevian opinion. The Irish produced good crops, and became men to appeal to, to depend on, to respect and to imitate. Increasingly young men of the tribes went across to the religion, and they served their purpose in educating their fathers. Moreover, the monks within the monastery appeared to combine health and apparent happiness with complete rejection of all forms of aggression. They were not weaklings; their daily routine was the toughest any man could keep to consistently all his life. So new meanings were read into a religion that seemed at first perverse. For almost the first time on the Continent, Christianity began to appeal to peasants and countrymen".[93]

At first the Irish settlers did not have the language skills to speak with the local people and, even when they learnt the language, there would still have been little understanding of the doctrine which they preached. However, their lifestyle began to impress the neighbours and as they cleared the forests to make room for agriculture around Luxeuil and drained the marshes to cultivate the land around Fontaines, people were attracted to them, to their message and finally to their God. So, whatever his own primary motive might have been, it is clear that Columbanus' monasticism did foster the spread of Christianity. This continued long after his death because each of his communities in France, Switzerland and Italy became places from where missionaries went forth.

A different type of missionary outreach was that initiated by Pope Gregory. Bede tells us that in 596 AD, Gregory,

> *"Being moved by Divine inspiration, in the 14th year of the same Emperor [Maurice], and about the 150th after the coming of the English into Britain, sent the servant of God, Augustine, and with him several other monks, who feared the Lord, to preach the word of God to the English nation".*[94]

By "English" Bede is referring to the Anglo-Saxon invaders who infiltrated the eastern side of Britain, driving to the west the Britons who were already there. Pope Gregory's initiative was something unique. "Gregory opened a new world to the papacy. This was the first papal mission to a pagan people".[95] Gregory firmly believed that the gospel was to be universal and declared in a sermon that, "God has made the preaching of the saints go out into all parts of the world – the east, the west, the south and the north".[96]

Again, there is frustratingly little information regarding the methods which Augustine and his group used to evangelise the people of Kent, but we do know that he went first to the king, Æthelberht. Bede tells us that in 597 AD the party from Rome landed on the island of Thanet just off the Kentish coast from where they sent a message to the king via Frankish interpreters. The king was to be informed that they came from Rome, "and brought a joyful message, which most undoubtedly assured to those who responded to it everlasting joys in heaven and a kingdom that would never end with the living and true God".[97]

Even though his wife was a Christian, the king remained suspicious and fearful, requesting the missionaries to stay on the island. However, a few days later he came to the island and met them. Having heard Augustine preach the king replied,

> *"Your words and promises are very fair, but as they are new to us, and of uncertain import, I cannot consent of them so far as to forsake that which I have so long observed with the whole English nation. But because you*

are come from far as strangers into my kingdom, and, as I conceive, your desire is to impart to us those things which you believe to be true, and most beneficial, we desire not to harm you, but will give you favourable entertainment, and take care to supply you with all things necessary to your sustenance; nor do we forbid you to preach and gain as many as you can to your religion".[98]

They were then given permission to come and reside in Canterbury, the king's capital and their mission appears to have seen quick success. In July 598 AD, Pope Gregory wrote to his friend Eulogius, Bishop of Alexandria, that in England "more than ten thousand are reported to have been baptised".[99] The king was also converted and so it may well be that, even if these numbers are not exaggerated, many of the reported conversions were superficial, "a tribal conversion".[100] However, Bede's description paints a picture of genuine Christian living and ministry having a real converting effect on ordinary people as well as on the king and other civic leaders. He asserts that as soon as Augustine and his companions entered Canterbury,

"They began to imitate the manner of life practiced in the primitive Church; applying themselves to constant prayer, watchings and fastings; preaching the word of life to as many as they could; despising all worldly things, as not concerning them; receiving only their necessary food from those they taught; living themselves in all respects conformably to what they taught, and being always ready to suffer any adversity, and even to die for that truth which they preached. In brief, some believed and were baptised, admiring the simplicity of their blameless life, and the sweetness of their heavenly doctrine".[101]

This picture may be idealised but, nevertheless, it presents a contrasting image as to how the Church grew within the Empire during this period. In fact, this picture of a small group of Christians living a distinctive lifestyle looks much more like how the Church grew during the second and third centuries.

It is interesting that, at least at the beginning, Pope Gregory expected the people to be converted in a much more formal and controlled way. He wrote to Bertha, King Æthelberht's wife, that although she should have already brought her influence to bear securing the king's conversion to Christianity, now is the time to make up for that missed opportunity so that she could encourage his conversion "and so kindle his heart even for the fullest conversion of the nation subject to him".[102] So, as Markus concludes, based on Gregory's letter, "the imperial model is again invoked to teach the same lesson: a true Christian ruler will promote and enforce the faith among his subjects".[103]

In a later letter after Æthelberht's conversion, Gregory exhorted him to "put down the worship of idols, overturn the edifices of their temples".[104] Yet, it appears that Gregory had second thoughts because, in a letter written to the Abbot Mellitus in Francia before he went to England, Gregory asked Mellitus to inform Augustine that he has,

"Long been considering in my own mind concerning the matter of the English people; to wit, that the temples of idols in that nation ought not to be destroyed, but let the idols that are in them be destroyed; let water be consecrated, and sprinkled in these temples, let altars be erected, and relics placed there. For, if those temples are well built, it is requisite that they should be converted from the worship of devils to the service of the true God; that the nation, seeing that their temples are not destroyed, may remove error from their hearts, and knowing and adoring the true God, may the more freely resort to the places with which they have been accustomed".[105]

Based on this evidence, Wood concludes that Gregory had come to think "that it was better missionary strategy to allow continuities between paganism and Christianity than to effect a complete break".[106] Furthermore, Bede asserts that coercion was never used in the conversion of the English and that even when King Æthelberht was converted he,

"Compelled none to embrace Christianity, but only showed more affection to the believers, as to his fellow citizens in the kingdom of Heaven. For he had learned from those who had instructed him and guided him to salvation, that the service of Christ ought to be voluntary, not by compulsion".[107]

So clearly, the context and method of mission is different here than within the Empire. Markus summarises,

"All his assumptions and a long tradition of thought about the duties of Christian rulers had combined to suggest Gregory's first response to the situation in England as he understood it: coercion by a Christian ruler.

That was the policy he had himself advocated elsewhere; and this was the response that came instinctively to his mind. He only came to question this strategy when the impossibility of applying it in the present case became starkly evident to him. That he did so is powerful testimony to Gregory's pastoral flexibility and constitutes a dramatic change of direction in papal missionary strategy".[108]

Nevertheless, although it seems there was no coercion, the progress of Christianity in the kingdom of Kent did advance much more easily because the king was supportive.

ORDINARY PEOPLE

We have been analysing the methods used by 'professional missionaries' be they monks or itinerant evangelists. Meanwhile, it is important to stress that their efforts were certainly not the only means by which the Christian message was taken beyond the boundaries of the Roman Empire. As ordinary Christians travelled, for a variety of reasons, they shared Christ as they went. The news of Jesus travelled with merchants, fugitive slaves, soldiers returning home after serving in the Roman army and captives to name but a few. However, as already noted, such people tend not to leave records or to have their biographies recorded by others.

Another means by which the Christian message spread was due to the fact that the vast majority of the peoples within the eastern part of the Empire spoke neither Latin nor Greek, but shared their language with the people on the other side of the border. For example, "numerous Syrians and Armenians lived in Persian dominated areas and were in constant touch with compatriots within Roman borders".[109] Sometimes, however, the spread of Christianity eastwards was for reasons much less peaceful than expatriates keeping in touch with their homeland.

In the ongoing wars between the Persians and the Romans, when the Persians had a success they often deported large numbers of people from the eastern borders of the Roman Empire into their own territory.[110] It is reasonable to assume that some of these deportees were Christian, but we have no specific records regarding most of them. Nevertheless, this section will attempt to draw together whatever evidence is available that can offer any insight into the contribution to the spread of Christianity made by ordinary Christian people. The vast majority of such people will remain anonymous forever.

The first reliable evidence of Christianity in Georgia comes from the *Ecclesiastical History* of Rufinus composed around 403 AD.[111] It tells the story of a Christian slave woman named Nino who caused the healing of a sick child and then, subsequently, the Queen of Georgia when she placed them on her hair shirt and prayed for them. Later the king was also converted through Nino. However, an interesting aspect of Rufinus' account is that, long before the miraculous is mentioned, he speaks of how Nino's lifestyle had impressed people.

"[Nino] lived among them and led such a full, sober and modest life, spending all of her days and nights in sleepless supplications to God that the very novelty of it began to be wondered at by the barbarians. Their curiosity led them to ask what she was about. She replied with truth: that in this manner she simply worshipped Christ as God. The answer made the barbarians wonder only at the novelty of the name, although it is true, as often happens that the very perseverance made the common women wonder if she were deriving some benefit from such great devotion".[112]

The fact that a devoted Christian life impressed people has a ring of authenticity about it, and I would suggest that, although many historical accounts emphasise the miraculous, the daily life of ordinary Christians probably led more people to Christ.

Many Indian Christians today still affirm a tradition regarding a Nestorian merchant called Thomas of Cana who landed in India around 345 AD bringing with him a group of Christian families. The traditions, while persistent, are unreliable and unclear, but the existence of so many strands does give us evidence that traders and other travellers played a leading role in the spread of Christianity east from Persia.

In addition to Christian merchants taking Christianity to far flung places, the reverse could also occur where a non-Christian merchant travelled to a location where there were already Christians, be converted and then return home to share his new faith. The *Chronicle of Seert* gives an example of just such an occurrence. A merchant from lower Arabia (present day Yemen) travelling on a business trip to Constantinople returned via Persia where he met a group of Nestorian Christians and was converted. He returned home to enthusiastically evangelise, beginning with members of his own family, but going on to carry the gospel into other surrounding Arab regions.[113]

Since the trade routes between China and Persia ran through what is now Iran and Afghanistan, it is not surprising that Christianity seems to have spread there at an early stage.[114] Bardaisan of Edessa wrote around 196 AD of Christians on the shores of the Caspian Sea.[115] However, we know almost nothing about how these Christian communities came into being. Syriac texts often mention when certain areas were absorbed into the Church structures of the East Syrian Church, but they do not give any information of how these Christian communities developed.[116]

The earliest record giving any detail of mission in these areas comes from an account written in the middle of the sixth century.[117] It describes how around 498 AD the Sasanian King Kawad (or Kavad) was overthrown and fled his own land seeking refuge amongst the Western Turks, known as Huns. The *Chronicle of Seert* records that King Kawad, "was benevolent towards the Christians, because the company of them rendered service to him on his way to the king of the Turks".[118] The document further describes how some of these Christians followed King Kawad into exile. John of Resh'aina and Thomas the Tanner are mentioned. When the king returned home after two years they remained, living there for more than 30 years having married and had children.

The first historically reliable information of the origin of Christianity in what was then the Kingdom of Aksum (now the Tigray region of Ethiopia) describes the faith coming from Tyre in Syria by way of the Red Sea. The Church historian Rufinus tells the story of Meropius, a Christian from Tyre, who was returning from a voyage to India with his nephews Adesius and Frumentius in the mid-340s AD. They stopped at a harbour on the eastern coast of what is now Eritrea just after the inhabitants of that city had broken their commercial treaty with the Romans. This meant there was no Roman protection and all the adults on the ship were massacred. The two young men were sold into slavery to the king of Aksum. Adesius became the king's cupbearer, while Frumentius' abilities were recognised and he was made steward of the king's wealth.

The king died when his son was too young to reign and so the queen mother asked the two young men to assist in administrating the land. This enabled Frumentius to support Christian traders who arrived and to provide them with a site where a church could be built. Eventually the two were released and while Adesius went back to Syria, Frumentius travelled to Alexandria where he visited the patriarch of the time, Athanasius.

In speaking of the young Church in Aksum, Frumentius requested that a Bishop be sent to nurture the Christians there. Athanasius responded by consecrating Frumentius himself and sending him back as Bishop.[119] Although this story might sound like a romantic tale, there is strong evidence for its historicity. A letter has been found written from the Arian Emperor Constantius to the then King of Aksum urging him to find an Arian Bishop rather than the Bishop supplied by Athanasius.[120] Frumentius then returned to Ethiopia where he was known as Bishop Salama and acted as a missionary Bishop.

Ethiopian tradition credits him with causing the conversion of the royal household, planting churches, ordaining priests, opening a school and translating portions of Scripture into the ancient Ethiopian language.[121] The king's conversion has been confirmed by the discovery of an inscription dated around 350 AD detailing a military excursion, but which begins and ends with an invocation to the Christian God.[122]

A little further north, between Ethiopia and Egypt, was the region of Nubia. Christianity travelled up the Nile to this region aided by the efforts of monks from Egyptian monasteries who took Christianity into the Nubian countryside.[123] However, the conversion of the ruling family of Nubia came about through the initial involvement of the Roman Emperor Justinian, or more particularly his wife Theodora. She received a petition from a Coptic priest named Julian who persuaded her to send missionaries to Nubia. In the event she sent Julian to spend two years in Nubia during which the king and his aristocracy were baptised.[124]

So, in Ethiopia we see the royal family converted through ordinary Christians who became missionaries when they arrived as captives in a strange land, while the royal family of neighbouring Nubia was converted through a Christian 'professional' sent by the Roman Empress.

Earlier we discussed the mission of Ulfilas to the barbarians across the Danube. However, a century before his time, Goths from the north-western shores of the Black Sea (at that time known as The Euxine Sea), developed ships which enabled them to cross the sea and raid the coastline of Asia Minor (modern Turkey). Not only did they carry off valuable items, they also took people into captivity either to make them slaves or in the hope that payment would be offered for their release.[125] In addition, these Goths travelled across the Danube into Thrace and the northern Roman provinces around the River Danube.[126] Again, people as well as treasures were taken captive and the Church historian Sozomen confirms that there were Christians among these prisoners and that, "the Barbarians, amazed at the conduct and wonderful works of these men, thought that it would be prudent on their part, and pleasing to the Deity, if they should imitate those whom they saw were better; and, like them, never end their homage to God".[127]

Sozomen's account that Christians were amongst those taken captive and that through them Christian faith was spread amongst the Goths is confirmed by another Church historian, Philostorgius (368-c439 AD), who was a native of one of the districts of Asia Minor which had been overrun and who wrote much nearer to the event. He describes how,

"A large multitude of Scythians, who lived north of the Ister, made an incursion into the Roman territory and laid waste a great part of Europe by their predatory excursions and afterwards having crossed over into Asia, invaded Cappadocia and Galatia. Here they took a large quantity of prisoners, among whom were not a few ecclesiastics; and they would return to their own country laden with spoils and booty. These pious captives, by their intercourse with the Barbarians, brought over a great number of the latter to the true faith, and persuaded them to embrace the Christian religion".[128]

We can only imagine the terrible suffering endured by these captives. But, nonetheless, the Christian faith did spread by means of these horrors.

Prosper of Aquitaine describes "some sons of the Church, made prisoners by the enemy, changed their masters into servants of the gospel". He also suggests that the reverse occurred, "some foreign pagans, whilst serving in the Roman armies, were able to learn the faith in our country, when in their own lands they could not have known it; they returned to their homes instructed in the Christian religion".[129]

As already discussed, Palladius and Patrick are the first named figures in Irish Christian history, but Christianity arrived in Ireland long before either of them. Proof of this is found in the *Chronicle* of Prosper of Aquitaine. Under the date 431 AD, Prosper records that "Palladius was consecrated by Pope Celestine and sent to the Scots [Irish] believing in Christ, as their first bishop".[130] So, clearly Prosper understood that there was already a sufficient number of Christians in Ireland by then to justify sending a bishop as it was completely unknown in the ancient Church for a bishop to be sent to a place unless there was a Christian flock there for him to minister to.[131]

Wood suggests that, "in Ireland, trading and raiding came before mission, and indeed helped to create the mission field".[132] Christianity first arrived in Ireland by various means and through people whose names will never be known. While Ireland was never part of the Roman Empire, there were longstanding trading relations between Britain and Ireland. Even in the first century, Tacitus was aware that Ireland's harbours were known to the Roman authorities in Britain "through trading and merchants".[133]

Of course, there were also less peaceful types of contact. Pirates from Ireland were raiding the western seaboard of Britain from the third century onwards.[134] So, "It would have been strange indeed if, in the Irish raids, Patrick was the only Christian to have been carried off or the sole one of the captives to develop a feeling of responsibility for imparting their faith to those among whom they had been involuntarily thrown".[135] There is also some evidence of an Irish settlement in south-western Wales possibly dating back as early as the fourth century. In this area there are memorial stones inscribed with Irish names in the Ogham script.

Furthermore, there are place names with Irish influence in this region and a number of legends which may contain some historical truth about a fourth-century tribe called the Deisi who came from south-eastern Ireland to Wales. These settlers would have come into contact with Christianity because they were near neighbours of Caerleon-on-Usk where Aaron and Julius were martyred and they were also close to the Christian owned villas of Gwent and Glamorgan. So, it is reasonable to conclude with Fletcher that Christianity came to Ireland from southern Wales, again through the movements of ordinary people.[136]

CONCLUSION

In Chapter Three we saw how, in the Roman Empire after Constantine, people increasingly just drifted into Church because it became the thing to do. During the same centuries outside of the Empire this would rarely, if ever, have happened. Where Christianity was not the State religion, it had no special favour and could even face hostility. In this environment the Christians shared their message by being distinctive and by showing a positive alternative. This positive alternative was demonstrated both in the monastic communities which were increasingly established in pagan areas and also, in the distinctive lifestyle of ordinary Christian people who travelled beyond where Christianity was the State religion. Within the Empire, in the centuries after Constantine, Christianity became increasingly aligned to the general society, while outside the Empire during the same period Christians were very different from their surroundings.

5

Mission Today

CHRISTENDOM

During our examination of the methods of mission employed by the Church during the first six centuries of its existence, we have charted the radical change in context which the Church experienced after the conversion of Constantine. In this period, the Church moved from the margins to the mainstream of Roman society. Church and State became ever more linked and the Church often adopted a central position in society. State law increasingly reflected Church teaching and the State even became involved in coercing people to become Christians. Indeed, within a century of it being illegal to be a Christian, it became illegal to practice paganism.[1] These trends continued in the following centuries and what is commonly known as 'Christendom' developed. This word is used to describe the process by which, for over 1500 years, the Church was a lynchpin around which society revolved across Europe and subsequently in other parts of the world.[2] In Christendom, the Church and the government together played a part in guiding the nation. Church leaders often held huge sway over political leaders and society looked to the Church for guidance, not just on moral issues, but in almost every aspect of life.

During Christendom, across the Western world, the Church became the centre of each local community and more or less the whole population accessed their local church building for services and other events. Going to church on a Sunday became one of the norms of society. The Church's central place was further enhanced by its role in education. At times the Church was the main, or only, provider of schools. Even when the State also began to run schools, it often became a legal requirement that Christian religion be included in the syllabus. During the Christendom era, virtually the whole population of the Western world was aware of the basic teachings of Christianity and had at least some knowledge of the Bible.

In Ireland, Christendom began to develop when tribal rulers converted to Christianity and their subjects had little real choice but to follow them. After the Synod of Whitby (664 AD), this Celtic Christendom was transformed into mainstream Roman Christianity – "Catholic Ireland was born".[3] Ireland's third Christendom was imposed following the English Reformation under Henry VIII. But after the official disestablishment of the (Anglican) Church of Ireland in 1870 and the partition of Ireland in 1921, two distinct Christendoms developed on this island and the link between political leaders and Church leaders became particularly pronounced on both sides of the border.[4]

In the Republic of Ireland, the most notable example of this link is Archbishop John Charles McQuaid, the Roman Catholic Archbishop of Dublin from 1940 to 1972. He had great influence with political leaders, partly because of a lifelong friendship with Eamon De Valera, and many historians see McQuaid's influence in the Irish Constitution. In the late 1980s, historian J.J. Lee wrote,

"The Church is a bulwark, perhaps now the main bulwark of the civic culture…if religion were no longer to fulfil its historic civilising mission as a substitute for internalised values of civic responsibility, the consequences for the country, no less than for the church, could be lethal".[5]

Similar links between Church and State can be identified in Northern Ireland going back to the 1912 Ulster Covenant opposing Home Rule. Among the first signatories were the leaders of the main Protestant denominations. Signing in their own blood, they committed themselves "to stand by one another in defending, for ourselves and our children, our cherished position of equal citizenship in the United Kingdom".[6] Perhaps the most explicit link between Church and State in Northern Ireland was the pronouncement of Lord Craigavon, the first Prime Minister of Northern Ireland, during a parliamentary debate, "that in the South they boasted of a Catholic State. They still boast of the Southern Ireland being a Catholic State. All I boast of is that we are a Protestant Parliament and a Protestant State".[7] Indeed, during the first half of Northern Ireland's existence there was discrimination against Catholic people, for example, in employment and access to public housing. This helped to fuel the civil rights movement in the late 1960s.

CHRISTENDOM OVER

It is largely true that the Church's move into the mainstream of society after Constantine continued for another 1500 years across the Western world. However, in recent decades this situation began to change, often quite rapidly. Precisely when this began is a matter of debate; some suggest that it dates to the end of the 1914-18 World War. Also the timing of the change varies from country to country, but there is no doubt that in recent decades Christendom has been breaking down. Right across the Western world the values and teaching of the Church are becoming less and less influential on society.

Until recently Ireland was one of the least secularised countries in the Western world, but now the link between Church and society is disintegrating here too. In the 2018 Referendum on abortion, a 66% majority voted to remove the Constitutional prohibition on abortion even though most Christian Churches urged people to vote that it should remain. Another example of the reduced influence of the Church was the Marriage Equality Referendum of May 2015, in which 62% voted to allow marriage between two people of the same sex. This was the first time that a State anywhere in the world legalised same-sex marriage through a popular vote.[8] Again, most Churches argued against this, but it seemed that the more the Church urged people to vote in one direction, the more people voted in the other. As Fraser Hosford summarises, "Christendom cannot be rebuilt. Attempts to tell people what to do through public policy are not only doomed to failure, but are also arrogant, and only antagonise the people the church seeks to bless".[9]

We are now left in no doubt that the Church no longer has an automatic hearing in Irish society. Another remarkable indicator of this was a speech in Dáil Éireann in 2011 by the then Taoiseach Enda Kenny. Referring to the Report into how child sexual abuse allegations were dealt with in the Diocese of Cloyne, Kenny described what he called the "dysfunction, disconnection, elitism and narcissism that dominate the culture of the Vatican to this day".[10] Even one generation earlier it would have been unthinkable for an Irish government leader to make such comments.

In a recent survey of young adults (aged 19-25) in Ireland, 65% identified as Christian, which is surprisingly high, but only 13% described themselves as practicing Christians.[11] Another poll conducted in Ireland in 2007 mapped this change by comparing the difference in religious knowledge between 15-24 year olds and over 65s. The results were stark and the trend was clear. For example, 63% of the older age group knew that there are four Gospels in the New Testament compared with only 38% of the younger group, while 43% of the over 65s knew the first of the 10 Commandments compared with only 5% of the 15-24 year olds.[12]

Other countries have travelled further along this road. Describing the USA, Chuck Colson proclaims, "We no longer live in Jerusalem, where everybody knew who God is, even those who did not believe. We now live in Athens, where you might get a hundred different answers to the question 'Who is God?'"[13]

More and more this present age is described as post-Christendom – "The culture that emerges as the Christian faith loses coherence within a society that has been definitively shaped by the Christian story and as the institutions that have been developed to express Christian convictions decline in influence".[14] Writing in the British context, Stuart Murray helpfully summarises that post-Christendom results in a number of transitions for the Church:

- From the centre of society, to the margins.
- From majority, to minority.
- From control over society, to offering the Church's voice as one of many.
- From feeling at home in a culture shaped by the Christian story, to being more like aliens or exiles in a culture that is not Christian based.[15]

In this environment, people are less and less likely to come to church just because it is the norm. To become a Christian or even to 'go to church' is again becoming a counter-cultural action. People are more likely to hold the perception that the Church is boring or even irrelevant to their lives. It makes no sense then for the Church's message to the world to be something like – "come to us, meet Jesus and the Church will become the new focus of your life".[16] There is a ring of truth about Frost and Hirsch's comment,

> "By anticipating that if they get their internal features right, people will flock to the services, the Church betrays its belief in attractionalism...If we get our seating, our parking, our children's programme, our preaching and our music right, they will come. This assumes that we have a place in our society and that people don't join our Churches because, though they want to be Christians, they are unhappy with the product. The missional

Church recognises that it does not hold a place of honour in its host community".[17]

HISTORY REVISITED?

We can see that the list of transitions experienced by the Church in the Western world today leaves it in a place reminiscent of the Church during the first three centuries of its existence. The pre-Constantine Church was also a small minority on the margins of society with no political power and little influence. Indeed, it was often under threat from the authorities and was almost always at odds with the surrounding culture. There are many similarities between the situation in which the Church in the Western world today finds itself and that faced by the Church in the second and third centuries AD. However, the two contexts are not identical.

For one thing, the Church in the second and third centuries was growing; it was on an upward curve, while much of the Church in the Western world today is in decline. Also, the Church in the second and third centuries had little of the complicated structure and expensive buildings which the Church often has today. Nor was it bound by centuries-old traditions which are difficult to change. Even though the general society in the Western world has largely moved away from Christianity, it is not virgin soil for the gospel of Christ. Traces of Christendom remain scattered throughout post-Christendom culture. For example, even the most secular society will still revere the architectural treasure of an ancient cathedral. Similarly, vestiges of Christendom remain in literature, historical study, coinage, art and music.[18] Christendom is, therefore, still not far enough away from today's culture to remove any inoculation effect. As Murray summarises,

> *"Most assume that the gospel is a boring reaffirmation of establishment values; Christians are naive, hypocritical, judgemental and intolerant; evangelism is an invitation to add a religious veneer to life and guarantee preferential treatment beyond the grave; and those responding need only make small, usually negative, adjustments to their lives. Such 'good news' lacks newsworthiness and sounds unattractive".*[19]

Furthermore, in Ireland the Church struggles to break free from the damage caused through such travesties as the Mother and Baby Homes, Magdalene Laundries, clerical sexual abuse scandals and the vicious corporal punishment inflicted on generations of pupils in Church-run schools. As I write, I remember a recent conversation with someone I met for the first time, on a golf course. When he discovered what I did he asked about the congregation where I am currently based. As I explained the joy of the multi-cultural church family I serve he responded by remembering his experiences in school and commenting that any change would be better than what had gone before.

SO WHAT ARE WE TO DO?

How should we react to the fact that the Church is being confined to the margins of society; seen to be irrelevant by most and viewed with suspicion by many? In this environment, what should our posture be? Here are a few suggestions.

Do not try to turn the clock back

Christendom is more or less over. Let it go. We may look back fondly on the days when the Church and its message was listened to with respect but we cannot recreate that. Let us stop trying to be what we once were. Frost and Hirsch agree,

> *"It is time to move on and find a new mode of understanding and engagement with surrounding contexts. We can no longer afford our historical sentimentality, even addiction, to the past…The answer to the problem of mission in the West requires something far more radical than re-working a dated and unattainable model".*[20]

The demise of Christendom leaves the Church with a choice. We can mourn the past and lament our current standing or we can seek to move on.

Accept (even embrace and celebrate) our place on the margins

The voice of the church is much less likely to be heard by wider society than even a generation ago, as Fraser Hosford has memorably described in his book *Down With This Sort Of Thing*. The recent Covid-19 restrictions drove this fact home. The church was included in the list of 'non-essential services', which were closed for long periods during the pandemic. We already knew the voice of the Church was marginalised but now it is officially classified as 'non-essential'. We are no longer in the centre. But do we want to be?

Chapter 5

In Chapter Three, we saw what happened when the Church gained centre ground under Constantine. Irish history also teaches the dangers of the Church having civil and political power. History shows that when 'going to church' becomes a societal norm, it can weaken rather than strengthen real Christian discipleship. So, while we know that the Church in Ireland is (generally) getting smaller, I suggest that it will also get stronger. The Church before Constantine was smaller, poorer and more marginalised, yet it was healthier.

Stop fighting for our rights

After Constantine, the idea of forcing someone to be a Christian became increasingly acceptable. Coupled with this was the use of Imperial forces to destroy pagan temples and the adoption of State legislation to outlaw pagan practices. Any Christian who had authority over other people was expected to use that authority to make sure they were converted. As Augustine put it, Christian rulers should "make their power the handmaid of His majesty by using it for the greatest possible extension of His worship". [21]

There was little evidence of any mission strategy in the church during the first three centuries. After Constantine the strategy was coercion. Christians today will wonder how this could ever have been thought an appropriate means to bring people to faith. And yet, if we are honest, do we not see forms of coercion in our relatively recent history in Ireland? Who can doubt that irreparable damage has been done to people who were forced to go to church so that they could get into a certain school, work in a certain business or access better housing, to name a few examples?

After Constantine, we saw an increasing power union between the civic authorities and church leadership. Again, this will be familiar to students of recent Irish history. For decades, Unionists in Northern Ireland vocally resisted Dublin rule because they claimed that Dublin rule equated to Rome rule and, to an extent, they had a point. We now know that the Archbishop in Dublin often had significant influence on the decision-making process of leaders in Government. It is equally true that collusion took place between Protestant leaders and civic authorities in Northern Ireland.

As Christians today we cannot undo this history but, if we are to be effective in sharing Christ, we need to approach people in the opposite spirit to Christendom and its Irish manifestation. There is no place for the 'carrot and the stick' in evangelism.

After Constantine the Church acquired rights for the first time. Naturally, this was welcomed as preferable to persecution. However, we now understand that great damage can be done to the cause of Christ if the Church asserts its rights inappropriately. The recent Covid restrictions led to renewed discussion among Christians as to the rights of the Church. Some argued that the government had no business telling churches to close and that the Church had a right to keep buildings open for corporate worship. Others (including me) believed that it was crucial for us to identify with and abide by the same restrictions facing people around us because that is what it means to be incarnational.

Post-Constantine Church history highlights the dangers of the Church having too many rights. In Ireland today we need to be careful about claiming our rights because people have been so hurt by Church power in the recent past. Writing in VOX magazine Kevin Hargaden comments,

> *"Christians in Ireland, in the North and in the Republic, have had all the religious rights they could desire for generations, and it has not made their mission any more compelling…Rights can be good things and they should not be discounted. But they are not the force that gives our words and actions power. They are not the force that gives us permission to live out our faith".*[22]

Learn from pre-Constantine Christians
While not identical, the post-Christendom context of today's Church is similar enough to the context of the Church in the second and third centuries for us to learn from their methods of mission. Before Constantine, Christians were a small, marginalised and sometimes persecuted fringe group. Their existence was vulnerable and shaky, while they had little or no influence over the way the Empire was run or even in the administration of their local communities.

Yet, this Church grew through the attractive lifestyle that Christians demonstrated incarnationally, the quality of the Church's common life and their attempts to reach out to meet the social needs of others. So maybe we should focus on the same. There is hope.

Incarnational Church
In the second and third centuries there is little evidence of major preaching events or travelling evangelists drawing crowds of people to listen. Such events would often have been impossible with pressure from the authorities and fear of persecution. For similar reasons, the Church could not advertise its presence or be open and transparent so that enquirers could

simply turn up. Likewise today, though for different reasons, we can no longer expect people to respond to an advertised special service in a church building or even to an evangelistic event on neutral ground.

Now that the Church is no longer at the centre of society, people are much less likely to be attracted into Church buildings or to Christian events. Notice boards, websites and other publicity can play a part in informing people of events taking place in the church building, but their effect is already much decreased and is continuing to decline.

A few decades ago, large crowds gathered around the Custom House steps in both Dublin and Belfast to listen to Christian preachers, but it is hard to imagine this happening today. In fact, it is increasingly rare to see anyone stopping to listen to the occasional open-air preachers on Dublin's O'Connell Street, for example.

During most of the nineteenth and twentieth centuries thousands of people attended evangelistic rallies where great preacher-orators gave passionate evangelistic messages and invited people to make a personal response. Notable examples include D.L. Moody, Billy Graham, Luis Palau and the Irish version, W.P. Nicholson.

However, by the end of the twentieth century this method of evangelism seemed to become less effective in the Western world. In the early 1990s Bishop John Finney enabled 1000 recent converts in England to complete a questionnaire.[23] Of these only 4% said evangelistic events were the main factor in their conversion. This figure confirms similarly low numbers in earlier research.[24] Although I am not aware of any equivalent research for Ireland, the results would, most likely, be along the same lines.

The reasons why these attractional events are less relevant to mission today are quite different from the reasons in the second and third centuries. Then it was because the Christians had to keep a low profile in a potentially hostile environment. Today it is more to do with the fact that the Church is largely ignored and people would not be inclined to attend.

Nevertheless, although the reasons are different, the end result is much the same. In neither context is large scale evangelism or other forms of attractional mission likely to be effective. It is no longer enough to simply publicise church activities and expect outsiders to come in.

For example, in October 2002, in conjunction with the 'Power to Change' initiative, a congregation, of which I was Minister, distributed 1000 invitations in the immediate vicinity of its building in the suburbs of Cork city. The attractive leaflet invited anyone who was interested in an Alpha course (described on the leaflet as an introduction to Christian faith) to call a local landline number for details. There were no responses whatsoever even though all the homes were within a few hundred yards of the church building.

Kieran Beville (a Pastor and writer in Cork) correctly concludes that, "If individualism and relativism are features of contemporary culture then there is a great need for the Church to counter this by being incarnational and transforming communities".[25]

Mission today needs more than just local congregations meeting and inviting passers-by to come in. That is not to say Christians should not meet for fellowship, indeed they must, but, it is ever more necessary for the members of local Christian congregations to be visible as Christians outside the church.

As Finney puts it, "Even more urgently needed are means of helping non-church goers to discover God *outside* the church building".[26] As the Christendom era comes to an end the Church must be "not only inviting but infiltrating".[27] The Church's strategy needs to move from being invitational to incarnational.[28] To quote Halter and Smay, the Church has to be "deeply imbedded in the world".[29]

When congregations gather in church buildings the focus should be on preparing Christians to take the gospel of Christ with them when they leave the building. Now that the Church is increasingly on the margins, the emphasis of church services and other gatherings needs to be "on equipping their members to live authentic and attractive Christian lives and to share their faith".[30] This also means that some churches may need to look at reducing their activities so that members can have time to relate meaningfully with friends, neighbours, work colleagues and others outside the Church.[31] It is all too easy for Christians to end up having few, if any, non-Christian friends. This can be particularly true in bigger churches with extensive programmes where people spend the vast majority of their leisure time participating in church activities. Finney is right to ask,

> *"Are too many Churches so over busy with their internal life that the members do not even have time to look after their own family let alone love their neighbours? Friendship needs time. Every Christian needs to examine the right relation between time given to the life of the Church and that given to their family and friends".*[32]

In his research, Finney found that the vast majority of the 1000 new Christians he surveyed began their journey towards Christ because of the influence of a Christian friend or family member.[33] Quoting another survey, Howard Lewis cites a figure of 79% of recent converts to Christianity who said that the main factor in bringing them to Christ was meeting a Christian in their work place or some other setting.[34] In Belfast in the late 1990s Lewis summarises,

> *"Every survey carried out in recent years reveals the same truth, that the vast majority of people who come to faith, ascribe the single most important human element in their conversion to the impact of a Christian friend, neighbour, relative or work mate. We need to spend much time reminding ourselves of the potential of our own ordinary, simple lives, as we live in touch with God and with others".*[35]

In their seminal book, *The Shaping of Things to Come*, Frost and Hirsch develop the analogy of Christians as "fishers of people".[36] They argue that Christians should not be anglers just making occasional forays into enemy territory with the gospel trying to 'hook' someone before quickly retreating back to the safety of the Church. They prefer the image of a drift net whereby there is a loose web of Christians sprinkled all around the community so that "by creating a net of deep, loving friendship, more and more people will be swept into the community".[37]

Eric Swanson poses a key question for the Church of today, "will we remain outside of the community inviting people in or will we go to our communities, seeking to be a transforming agent?"[38] I am reminded of hearing Cardinal Murphy O'Connor (the then leader of the Roman Catholic Church in England) noting that Jesus gave two images for the church – a city on a hill and yeast in the dough[39] – before commenting that for most of the Church's history we have been the first, but now we need to be moving into the second, "being the community of Christ within wider society – touching lives on the ground".[40]

Now that the Church is marginalised, Christians must show or demonstrate the gospel and must live incarnationally in their surrounding communities to ensure that their demonstration of the gospel is witnessed by people outside. Christendom is over; the Church is no longer the city on the hill seen by everyone. Yet, from the margins, Christians can be effective yeast in the dough.

WHAT COULD THIS LOOK LIKE IN IRELAND TODAY?

In the Western world there is now little or no place for attractional models of mission. The only way people can encounter the Christian message is if the Church lives incarnationally, so that Christians can demonstrate Christ in their local environments. But is this generalisation specifically and entirely true for Ireland? Does a place for attractional mission remain in Ireland today? I have lived and worked in the Republic of Ireland for the past 25 years as well as for much of my childhood. So, my own experience forms most of the basis for the following observations.

The Mission Context in Ireland Today

In describing people in Ireland today in relation to the Church, the categories detailed in the Church of England report, "Mission-shaped Church" are helpful. This report placed the population of England (not including those who are members of other world faiths) in five categories:

- Regular Attenders – those who attended at least monthly.
- Fringe – those who attended Church less than once a month.
- Open De-Churched – those who attended Church at some point in their life who no longer do so, but would be open to return if the right contact was made.
- Closed De-Churched – those who attended Church at some point in their life, but who were damaged or disillusioned in some way and have no intention of returning.
- Non-Churched – those who have never been to Church, except perhaps for a funeral or wedding of a friend or relation.[41]

In Ireland today there are still very few "Non-Churched" people. Until recently the vast majority of the population attended services regularly. The Church has been so intrinsic to general society that it is almost inconceivable that anyone living here could not be aware of it and have some exposure to its public worship, as well as some understanding of its message.

However, in the last few decades there has been a huge increase in the number of "De-Churched" people. Many of these are "Closed De-Churched" because they have been put off by child abuse scandals, refusal to marry divorcees, an authoritarian attitude from their local clergy or some other reason. Others could be classified as "Open De-Churched". They have drifted away and got out of the habit of going to services, but given the right invitation or opportunity they may not object to returning. In fact, this often happens because most of the primary schools in the Republic of Ireland are under Church patronage and children are prepared for First Communion (in second class) and Confirmation (in sixth class). Parents who still see themselves as Catholics want their children to participate. Even if they have been out of the practice of going to church they tend to return around this time.

Another section of the population in Ireland no longer attend services and have fallen out with their Church, but have not fallen out with God. Many still engage in some form of personal prayer. Also, there has been a significant increase in interest in alternative spirituality. Many large towns and cities have "Mind, Body, Spirit" festivals where a bewildering array of spiritualities are on offer. Yet, a significant proportion of these people still want to maintain some form of Christian spirituality. They could be described as "Open De-Churched" in that, while they have rejected the Church they grew up in, they might well be open to some other Christian Church.[42] This is evidenced by the rise in small, often independent, evangelical fellowships that have sprung up during the last two decades or so.[43]

A further trend in Ireland is that, although attendance at mass has plummeted, baptism remains popular. An Irish Times family values poll conducted in 2015 concluded that, "While up to 93% of parents said they baptised their children, only a third of children were taken to mass regularly".[44] Although some argue that this is primarily about access to Church-run schools, the truth is more complicated. Fr Gerry O'Connor, a parish priest in Cherry Orchard, said baptism rates were extremely high in his parish even though access to over-subscribed schools was not an issue locally, "It's a tradition, a ritual. It's a way of bringing the family together. I think that's why we've an incredibly high turnout for baptisms".[45]

Commenting on the surprisingly high number of teens and young adults in the Republic of Ireland who identified themselves as "Christian" in the recent Barna survey, a young woman from Cork lamented, "People even now think that it's all about rituals, [when] it's all about relationship. People cling onto what the past has told them about our faith, but they don't actually know it for themselves".[46]

Murray describes many parts of the Western world as a "twilight zone between the demise of Christendom and the full development of post-Christendom".[47] In this zone the Church misses out on both of two possible advantages – "the freshness of the story in pre-Christendom or its familiarity in Christendom".[48] However, this is not altogether true of the Republic of Ireland.

There are significant numbers of people carrying some familiarity with the Christian story who have now drifted away from the Church they grew up in, yet are somewhat open to a fresh presentation of the Christian message. Halter and Smay write,

> *"When the values of church and culture are similar, it's much easier to create a common space for saints and sojourners to be together. This is why the traditional 'come to us' attraction model of church was successful in the past. People outside the church still appreciated our values".*[49]

Unwittingly, this is a major part of the reason why the attractional model still works to some extent in the Republic of Ireland. Despite widespread anger and disillusionment with the Church, there are still many broad similarities between the values of Church and of society. Therefore, some people are looking for a slightly different but orthodox Christian expression of Church, which, again, is part of the reason for the recent growth of historical Protestant denominations and new Church congregations in the Republic of Ireland.

Shifting Ground – a Case Study

Between 2002 and 2015, I either oversaw or was directly involved in the planting of new congregations in the South Kerry/North-West Cork area. In these congregations approximately half of the people come from other countries and are a product of the huge increase in immigration to Ireland during the last two decades, while the other half are made up of people who grew up in the Catholic Church before drifting away and subsequently finding a spiritual home in the Methodist Church. Nevertheless, it is not an easy or natural move for people who grew up in the Catholic Church in Ireland to start attending a Methodist Church.

The residual attachment to the Catholic Church goes deep and all the more so in rural areas such as Kerry and North Cork. This is because Ireland's political history caused the Catholic Church to become equated with Irish national identity. For someone who grew up Catholic to start attending another Church is a much bigger thing than simply changing denomination. For some it would almost seem an unpatriotic act. In addition, many who go to a different Christian Church having been previously part of a Catholic Church can face suspicion, disappointment and even animosity from their family. I related regularly with people who faced real anger in their extended family relationships because of their decision to practice their Christianity in a Methodist Church. This is not just because of history, but also because the Church continues to be so closely linked with Irish culture and the school system.

For example, one Sunday a member of a congregation in South Kerry brought her friend to a service. This (divorced) lady and her two sons so enjoyed the service and the sense of community in the congregation that they were virtually the last people to leave the building. However, a few days later, when her estranged husband heard about it, he absolutely forbade her to ever take his children there again. This man professed to be an atheist but was 'a Roman Catholic atheist'. Clearly his objections were not spiritual, but further investigation showed that his reaction was based on a fear that his sons would in some way be separated from the mainstream, even ostracised, particularly in school.

In listing some elements of New Testament teaching that had been important in pre-Constantine times but were then excluded or reinterpreted in Christendom, Murray said, "faith in Christ was no longer understood as the exercise of choice in a pluralistic environment where other choices were possible without penalty".[50] In many ways the environment in this part of Ireland is still not sufficiently pluralistic for choices to be made without penalty. It is not the Church that imposes this penalty but, rather, family and society pressures.

In this context then, the Methodist Churches in this area operate as attractional churches but also seek to be incarnational. The attractional model works for those who are seeking a living Christian faith but are not finding it in the Church they currently attend or have recently left. However, there is still a need for incarnational mission to build bridges with those who will never drift into church. A small proportion of these are completely "Non-Churched", but the majority are people who once were part of a Church and for whom attending another would be simply too big a step to take on their own. In my experience, they will only come because of what they have seen in the lifestyle of their friends or family members.

The image of a "centred-set church" which Frost and Hirsch describe is one I recognised in the Methodist congregations in South Kerry/North-West Cork.

"In a centred-set church it is recognised that we are all sinners, all struggling to be the best people we can be. But we also believe that the closer one gets to the centre (Christ), the more Christ-like one's behaviour should become. Therefore, core members of the church will exhibit the features of

Christ's radical lifestyle (love, generosity, healing, hospitality, forgiveness, mercy, peace, and more), and those who've just begun the journey toward Christ (and whose lives may not exhibit such traits) are still seen as 'belonging'. No-one is considered unworthy of belonging because they happen to be addicted to tobacco, or because they are not married to their live-in partner. Belonging is a key value. The growth toward the centre of the set is the same as the process of discipleship".[51]

I have seen core members of these congregations exhibit the Christ-like lifestyle described above, and do so incarnationally, so that people with little or no real connection to any Church can see it and be influenced towards Christ and the Church as a result.

There is also evidence of the "net of friendship" image described by Frost and Hirsch. They envisaged non-Christians who have a Christian friend increasingly being drawn into the Christian's friendship circles so that they get to know more Christian friends and come closer to the church community where they can then be influenced by at least one Christian with the gift of an evangelist. This principle was seen in practice in the Methodist Churches of South Kerry/North-West Cork where people were drawn into Christian circles through a net of friendships with Christians and then someone in the church gently led them towards a commitment to Christ. Yet this will usually only happen if people feel welcomed by the church community and if they sense that the worship and fellowship of the congregation is authentic.

In his study on the differences between Celtic and Roman mission in the first six centuries of the Church and their relevance for today, Finney concludes,

"When a large group of people are not Christian, living in a society which has attitudes and an ethos which is not Christian, then the Celtic model of evangelism is more effective…After the 'conversion' of a nation or community, when a 'Christendom' situation obtains, then a settled Roman pattern is more satisfactory…Where there is a 'mixed economy' – where Christendom still has some vestiges of its former glory… we need a mix of both Roman and Celtic forms of ministry. We need the stability of the parish system, but we need also the freedom and ability to experiment of the entrepreneurial evangelist".[52]

Chapter 5

The context for the Church in South Kerry/North-West Cork is in many ways such a "mixed economy" and the Methodist Churches there exhibit a combination of both attractional and incarnational mission. However, that combination only remains effective because the Church still has a significant presence in society. In many parts of the Western world this is no longer the case, so rendering attractional methods of mission almost irrelevant. In Ireland it seems likely that current trends will continue, resulting in attractional mission becoming less and less effective and incarnational mission becoming increasingly necessary. Let us explore this further with an example from my recent experience in Dublin.

In 2013, Dublin Central Mission initiated outreach work in the Ashtown area, which lies approximately halfway between the Mission's city centre congregation in Abbey Street and its congregation in Blanchardstown, planted in 2008. The Ashtown area has only been developed in recent years. Thousands of people recently came here to live, either in gated apartment blocks or newly-built town houses, but there was no worshipping congregation of any kind. Five families connected with the Abbey Street congregation were identified as living in or close to Ashtown and they met as a small home cell group from March to May 2013. In the Autumn of that year, a room was found to rent and a part-time church development worker appointed. Plans were drawn up to begin a weekly Sunday evening gathering and open-air summer camps were organised for the children of the area. Special events were also organised on occasions such as St. Patrick's Day, Good Friday and Christmas. Over 30 children attended the Summer Club in 2014 but by the end of that year the weekly services ceased because, while a few curious onlookers came, they failed to attract any new local members. In addition, emigration led to two key families leaving making the remaining numbers too low. Despite a significant financial investment and a high-profile presence in the area, no lasting connections were made. This was the situation I inherited on arrival at Dublin Central Mission in the summer of 2015.

Having just come from Kerry, I felt it was worth another attempt, this time based on a model which had produced some fruit in that area. This model required little or no financial investment and so could be sustained over the long term. In early 2016 we borrowed a room in a community centre and put up posters around the area advertising a monthly meeting for 'praise, prayer and Bible study'. In partnership with the management company, we were able to access the mailboxes of all of the people in the gated apartment blocks to distribute flyers.

A small group of us met faithfully for two years, but again, while one or two people who had some kind of church background came occasionally, it all petered out. So, was that it for Ashtown? The church development worker wrote in 2015, "If strategies for ministry cannot be established amongst young professionals, who are essentially post-Christian in practice and living in gated apartment blocks, then the church should probably pack up its bags and give up".[53]

Thankfully, that is not the end of the story. Just around the time that our services fizzled out a young man who I knew vaguely from my time in Kerry contacted me. He belonged to a Christian Church not far from Ashtown and, with his wife and young children, had come to live in a house right in the heart of the new development. He really sensed God's call to use his home as a base to plant seeds for the gospel. I was delighted to bless him in his work and continue to pray for him. At the time of writing (summer 2021) a core group has formed around this family and a few local people have become Christians and joined the group.

Plans are in place for what looks like will finally become a church plant in the Ashtown area. The key difference is that this latest work is based around a family who live in the same streets as the people that they are seeking to reach. To quote again from the development worker who finished work in 2015, "consciously or unconsciously Ashtown Methodist has operated from a framework of 'church planting'. Instead, the methodology should move from 'planting' to 'incarnating', from 'congregation' to 'mission', from 'gathering' to 'sending out'".[54] His words turned out to be prophetic as this is exactly what appears to be happening now.

During the period 2016/17 we had no choice but to attempt attractional mission in Ashtown because none of us lived anywhere near the area. We put up posters and rented a room hoping to attract some "Open De-Churched" people as a starting point. This had worked to some extent in Kerry and North Cork but it did not work in Ashtown. On reflection, I believe that the reason for this is that most of the population in Ashtown were closer to being "Non-Churched" than "De-Churched". In a place like Ashtown the vestiges of Christendom are almost gone. It seems that the attractional mode of mission will really only have any effect amongst people who have some kind of Church background and who see themselves as returning to the life of the Church rather than coming into it for the first time.[55]

Another reason why some attractional mission might still work in Ireland is the recent arrival of peoples who have migrated here from countries where the church is strong. When they arrive, they go looking for a church and often will seek out denomination names that are familiar.

During late Spring 2021, in the first few weeks of in-person services after a winter of Covid restrictions, we welcomed several families and individuals who came originally from other countries, turning up for the first time having searched on the internet for a Methodist Church in Dublin. Indeed, this has been the story of Abbey Street Methodist Church for the last two decades. In the late 1990s it had become very small and the remaining faithful members wondered if they should give up travelling into the city centre for worship. However, they felt a clear calling to remain in the city. Soon after people began to migrate to Ireland and the church grew. Abbey Street is now a multi-ethnic congregation full of committed Christian people who have come from across the globe.

There was a similar story in the Methodist Church in Longford, the first place I was based as an ordained Minister from 1997-2002. When I arrived there the congregation was largely made up of several generations of the same families but, towards the end of my time, two local hostels became Direct Provision centres. A few years later Longford became popular as an affordable place where new Irish residents could rent housing. The last time I visited the congregation I did not know many of the people and they had their roots from all over the world.

CONCLUSION

There remains some place for attractional mission in Ireland today; namely in areas where there are likely to be "De-Churched" people and amongst people who have recently migrated from countries where the church is thriving. However, there are increasing numbers of contexts in Ireland where attractional mission will not attract. For now, mission in Ireland can be a mixture of attractional and incarnational, but the days of attractional mission having any effect are already over in some areas (such as Ashtown) and are numbered everywhere. A quotation from the seminal study by the Church of England, "Mission-Shaped Church", is instructive,

> "The missionary situation faced by the Church has changed. Inviting people back to Church as we currently know it may be an effective mission strategy for reaching up to (perhaps) one third of the population who are de-Churched. It is misconceived to assume that this represents a coherent mission approach for the majority of the population for whom Church as we know it is peripheral, obscure, confusing or irrelevant".[56]

Here in Ireland, there are now more and more people "for whom Church as we know it is peripheral, obscure, confusing or irrelevant", as well as many more for whom Church has been hurtful and untrustworthy. Therefore, if Christians are to effectively share our message with others we need to "see the incarnation of Jesus as a call for the Church to leave its 'safe' building and move into the world".[57] The primary method of mission of the early church was to "take care that there emerged everywhere in the world communities of disciples in which Jesus' praxis of the reign of God is lived in radical faithfulness to Jesus".[58] The church of today must do the same.

6

Mission from the Margins

We still have a mission. Our methods must change, but let us not give up hope – God still calls us to follow Him in His mission – we can do this, in His strength. There are ways of reaching people in Ireland today even if they are unlikely to just show up in our churches of their own accord. By combining lessons from the earliest Christians living on the margins of Roman society and Christians around Ireland today, this chapter will offer some illustrations of the possibilities.[1]

HOSPITALITY

Private homes played a pivotal role in the early growth of the Church as the message was largely disseminated by normal social networks and extended family circles. The place of the home is again becoming increasingly important for mission today. Nowadays, one of the key front lines of the church is the street (or townland) where a Christian lives. We have to find ways of using natural neighbourly hospitality to enable people to catch a glimpse of the good news of Christ. In general, Irish homes are less open than they were a generation ago. In times past, communities tended to be more stable with the same families growing up in the same street. Neighbours were in and out of each other's houses and front doors were rarely locked. Now though, people move around more so that, while we may still know our immediate neighbours to wave at, that is often as far as it goes.

During the Covid-19 restrictions there were long periods when people could not visit inside each other's homes. Yet, ironically, during this same time neighbours got to know each other better because they made more of an effort to look out for one another, perhaps to help with shopping or, in good weather, to sit out in front for a chat across the road. The images we saw during the Covid lockdowns of things like informal keep-fit classes in the street raise all kinds of possibilities for Christians. The two and five kilometre restrictions of 2020 and 2021 meant people spent more time in their own immediate neighbourhood rather than simply using their home as a dormitory from which to travel somewhere else for work.

I think, for example, of one young mother in County Armagh who, by dropping a note through the doors of the houses in her street, created a WhatsApp group which then became a network of mutual support for the neighbourhood. The impact of Christians involved in such missional initiatives cannot be under-estimated. Loneliness is on the increase in Ireland as people keep themselves to themselves. Christians would do well to be watchful for new people moving into the area who may well be looking for some friendly contact. A cup of coffee or even a meal can go a long way in forming relationships and in presenting Christ through the medium of hospitality.

A different example of the effective use of a home comes from my time in Co Kerry. We identified a regional town where there was little or no evangelical witness, rented a well-known location in the town and put up posters advertising a meeting for prayer, praise and Bible study. Although there were some encouraging signs initially, it petered out within a few months. Nevertheless, there was one local lady who came to saving faith in Christ and ended up coming to our other church 25 kilometres away. A couple of years later she invited me to visit her home and said something like "I see my friends where I was and I want them to have what I have found. If I get them here will you come?" What a dream invitation for a preacher. A few weeks later we gathered in the house with people filling the front room, the hallway and even sitting up the stairs. The difference between this meeting and the meetings two years previously was the personal involvement of a key local person and her home.

Another historical precedent for hospitality as mission is seen in the monasteries. Having said that, as discussed in Chapter Four, early monks generally had no real missionary intention as they withdrew to remote places so that they could focus on a life of devotion to God. However, as more and more of these solitaries came together and formed communities, they ended up having a part to play in impacting others towards Christianity. Some of the monasteries became places of sanctuary for fugitives and of rest for travellers. As this ministry of hospitality increased it is easy to envision people being attracted to Christian faith.

Chapter 6

Hospitality can be an important offering of the church today. In our church buildings we need to find ways of presenting an open door to passers-by. Both in Kerry and more recently in Dublin, I have been part of churches that host weekly coffee events where the door is literally left open for anybody to come in and sit around the table, with no strings attached, just to enjoy a cup of coffee, a scone and as much (or little) conversation as they want.

Having said that, the numbers have generally been small and, while those who do come in appreciate the company, we need to find ways of making our 'doors' seem more open. The threshold of a church door seems high to many Irish people. If someone wants to go to a service then they will go into a church building, but it will not necessarily cross their mind to do so for any other reason. So, we need to find ways of declaring to those who no longer want to go near a church service that they are still welcome in the building, even if it is just for a cup of coffee. Of course, the most effective way of doing this is by a personal invitation from their Christian friend.

One further development of hospitality ministry is to bring it outdoors into the grounds of our churches, where possible. In both Cork and Kerry, churches I was linked with hosted wonderful family days including bouncy castles, music and free refreshments. In Killarney it was on St Patrick's Day when the town was full and the parade passed the gates while in Cork it was in high summer. In both places substantial numbers of people willingly spent time with us. I remember interesting conversations with those who felt they should be paying for the refreshments but we insisted everything was free. This became an effective way of demonstrating and discussing grace. I was reminded of this again recently while reading Robert Holden's description of the "Loaves and Fishes Café" in Arklow. "The simple act of kindness struck people at the heart level too, with several saying that they were not used to experiencing that".[2]

As I write this (in summer 2021) we are being encouraged by the government to have an outdoor summer and lots of imagination and expense has gone into creating spaces for outdoor dining and socialising. Even in winter, during the Covid restrictions, we saw families gathering for birthday parties in car-parks and people bringing deck chairs and umbrellas to share takeaway coffee together. There are church congregations meeting for worship in their grounds rather than in their building or gathering in the local park, reminiscent of "they continued to meet together in the temple courts".[3]

So, notwithstanding the Irish weather, here is an opportunity for churches to ask how they can make more use of the outdoors to lower the 'threshold' for people who might never enter a church building.

In thinking about hospitality let us also remember that a church does not need to have a building to offer hospitality any more than an individual Christian must have a home before they can offer hospitality. Jesus practiced hospitality even though he had no home of his own. Hospitality is an attitude.[4] It includes taking someone for coffee, going for a drive in the mountains, arranging a game of golf, whatever.

An attitude of hospitality also demands that we are open to our schedules being disrupted so that we can give time to someone who needs it. As Rosaria Butterfield puts it, "Practicing radically ordinary hospitality necessitates building margin time into the day, time where regular routines can be disrupted".[5]

The Covid-19 pandemic has resulted in many people working from home. This suits some but leaves others feeling isolated. Many churches have rooms which are little used during the week. Could these be used to offer a co-working space to people who live close by and no longer commute somewhere else to work; using a resource we have to facilitate community amongst at-home workers who are seeking company?[6] Furthermore, not only can churches offer physical space for co-working, we also have the potential to enable those who use the space to encounter something of the love of God.

A further aspect of hospitality which churches can explore and which parallels with some of the monasteries 1500 years ago is the idea of the church offering sanctuary. The church where I am currently based in Dublin has just been registered as a 'Church of Sanctuary'. This is part of a network in Ireland sharing the objective of promoting a culture of welcome and inclusiveness, offering people somewhere to go where they can feel safe and be welcome.[7] This is particularly aimed at offering sanctuary to people who are fleeing violence and persecution. It is an attempt to actively 'welcome the stranger'.

Another example is the 'Safe Church' initiative, which aims to empower churches to provide a safe place for anyone affected by domestic violence or abuse. This includes offering confidential access to relevant information and support.[8] Of course, all of the above is a far cry from travellers turning up at a fifth century monastery in the Egyptian desert. Surely there is no modern equivalent for this – or is there?

In post-modern Ireland there are growing numbers of people looking to escape the whirlwind of modern life even for a short time. Lots of different faiths and other groups offer retreat centres, while Christian monasteries in Ireland are finding themselves a source of interest once again. These monasteries were not necessarily established for evangelistic reasons but have ended up welcoming people seeking an escape from modern life, who end up seeking God.

AUTHENTIC LIFESTYLE

"People today are weary of words...the focus moves from the credibility of the faith, that something is deemed true intellectually speaking, to the plausibility of the faith, that something is experienced as true in the way we live".[9]

Recently, someone I had only just met asked a question which took me aback. On hearing that I was a Minister in the Church he enquired whether faith was real for me or if it was just a job. I knew he meant no offence and that he was simply enquiring which of two perfectly possible options described me. I responded that Jesus was my life and that I was a Christian first and foremost; the fact that I worked for the Church was secondary to that. "So, you have that peace then" he replied in a way that suggested he did not but would quite like to. I came away wondering if he was one of the "many who have abandoned the church precisely because they did not perceive it to be spiritual enough".[10]

After Constantine, church services became big, polished and public. Huge and magnificently ornate church buildings were constructed and worship services became increasingly sophisticated. In conjunction with worship becoming more elaborate and formal, it also became almost exclusively dominated by clergy. It is possible that this grandeur impressed people towards Christianity, but it seems more likely that it made congregations feel rather remote from what was going on at the front of the church. Congregations became spectators rather than participants. These services drew large crowds so that the massive buildings were well filled, but attendees were more and more non-participatory audiences watching the 'professionals' at work.

The recent history of the Irish church has followed a similar track. We have seen a model of church where people come to sit or stand as instructed while watching a small number of people at the front do what they do so expertly. The result can be a sense of disenfranchisement generated in non-participatory spectators who eventually drift away because they no longer see a reason to be there.

During the first three centuries, Christians were often deemed to be somewhat strange whereas, after the conversion of Constantine 'going to church' became the norm and people attended services for all kinds of reasons. There were social, commercial and political advantages to going to church. At the upper levels of society anyone who wanted to progress in their career needed to be seen at services and it became fashionable to be a Christian. This all led to the development of a mindset that the church was there to serve the members or what today we may call the attitude of 'consumer Christians'.

This idea of the church existing to serve those who attend will be familiar to anyone who has lived in Ireland during the last century. We know that Christians are called to serve Christ and the Church, not the other way round, but the feeling persists that our needs and even wishes ought to be supplied and fulfilled by the church.

There are two consequences of this. For many who still attend there can be an often sub-conscious feeling that they are rather good to do so; the church should be grateful for their attendance, even owing them something in return. The other consequence is people leaving the church because they feel it has let them down or has not 'delivered' for them in the way they thought it should.

In the centuries after Constantine, the Church was no longer solely comprised of convinced believers who had made a conscious and perhaps sacrificial commitment, and so Christian lifestyle often became indistinguishable from the rest of society. In contrast, many historical sources quoted in Chapter Two describe a Christian lifestyle that was quite distinct from the lifestyle of those around them. The argument is clearly presented by Apologists and other writers that this is a key sign of the truth and effectiveness of Christianity.

It is also clear that, following the lead of later New Testament teaching,[11] the Church leaders of the second and third centuries constantly taught that Christians should live out their faith so that their lifestyle would be a positive advertisement for Christianity. The leaders of the Church were convinced this was crucial for mission. Christians in Ireland today need to face the fact that people are now much less likely to come to us, so we must go to them and we must demonstrate our faith by showing a distinctive and attractive lifestyle.

In the writings of Paul, there are surprisingly few direct exhortations to his churches to be actively involved in mission. There is nothing equivalent to the commissions which Jesus gave to his followers in, for example, Matthew 28:19-20, John 20:21 and Acts 1:8. On the other hand, Paul's letters are full of ethical injunctions, instructing and cajoling his readers regarding how they should live. Is this really so surprising though?

In these early years of the Church when everyone was a recent convert, people would have been instinctively inclined to tell others about their faith, so they did not need to be instructed to do so. But it was important for Paul to make sure that the lifestyle of his congregations would back up their verbal witness.[12] "Paul is not a moralist telling Christians how to behave. He is a missionary pastor and theologian who never tires of explaining the Christian message and of instructing Christians concerning areas in their lives in which the truth of this message makes a difference".[13]

Words such as those found in Colossians 4:5-6 are reminders that mission is clearly understood as the responsibility of the whole church, not just the travelling evangelists like Paul. "Be wise in the way you act towards outsiders; make the most of every opportunity. Let your conversation be always full of grace, seasoned with salt, so that you may know how to answer everyone".

Commenting on this passage Bowers points out,

"The local congregation is here clearly seen in an evangelistic role, even though it must at once be noted for the sake of precision that this role is not on the pattern of Paul's own work. It is a ministry of attraction and responsiveness rather than one of deliberate outreach and active solicitation. If it may be put that way, it is a stationary rather than a mobile witness. But it is a witness".[14]

That phrase, "a stationary rather than a mobile witness" resonates with me when I think of mission in Ireland today. If people are to encounter Jesus as good news, they need to see Christian living modelled consistently in the lives of their friends and neighbours. Irish people generally do not respond well to a 'smash and grab' encounter. We are more likely to watch for a while before engaging with something new. In my experience this is especially the case in rural communities and small towns. Many missionaries/church planters in Ireland today will testify that nothing much happened for some time after they started out in a new area until trust was built, which often took years.

Just recently I heard of a lady who arrived into a local church with her daughter. It turned out that she was a health-care provider for one of the congregation, a former work colleague of another and a regular coffee-mate of a third. None of them had invited her to church but their lives displayed a quality that eventually made her curious enough to check out their church, and she stayed.

Another similarity between today's Church and that of the pre-Constantinian period is that basic Christian theology is largely incomprehensible to those outside the Church. One of the features of our times is a rejection of the idea of absolute truth. Instead it is believed that truth is subjective and what is true for you may or may not be true for me. This compares with the pre-Constantine period when people in the Roman Empire usually believed in different gods and were quite open to the idea of adding another god to their faith collection. As Finney puts it, "The pagan world was unbelievably complicated: myth piled on myth so that even today we cannot find coherence or a unifying theme".[15]

Conversely, the early Christians were completely uncompromising in the basic tenets of their theology. They believed that their message was unique and that it was good news for all the world. From this starting point then,

> *"The early preachers did not enter into dialogue with the world, except to understand it and to present their life-changing message in terms comprehensible to their contemporaries. They believed they had got good news for their friends, and they knew that that good news was embodied in Jesus Christ. Him they proclaimed".*[16]

The Christians were unique in their day in declaring that anyone who became a servant of Christ also needed to reject all other gods. This idea of complete conversion and rejection of other faiths was virtually unknown in the world of the Roman Empire.[17]

MacMullen notes that stories of miracles performed by other deities were circulated just as much as stories of Christian miracles and they also had the effect of bringing people to believe in these other gods but, "These new devotees were thenceforth not lost to paganism. They only focused a particular conviction and gratitude on one more god. Christian converts, by contrast, denied the name and even the very existence of all those gods, from the moment of believing".[18] In this context the exclusivist claims of

Christians were a hurdle which would have been difficult for people of that time to jump.

Wilken also notes the comment of a Roman pro-counsel at the trial of a Christian in North Africa that "if you make fun of things we hold sacred I will not allow you to speak".[19] Green correctly observes that the early Christians' acknowledgement of only one God and their advocacy of the need for a total surrender to him, "was flying in the face of all conventional social propriety".[20]

We can draw a parallel to post-modern Ireland, which proclaims that belief or faith is personal and that whatever you believe is valid and true so long as you believe it. To put it another way, post-modernism embraces a pantheon of gods and people are happy just to add another god to their list.

Yet the Christians in the early centuries of the Church held unswervingly to the unique lordship of Christ, even though they lived in a context just as pluralist as ours, maybe even more so. The key point to note is that their lifestyle often won people over before their message did. That also is the challenge for us today. As Joel Edwards puts it, "Our value as citizens should be judged not by what we say about Jesus but by our acts of kindness which serve everyone indiscriminately".[21]

In the early centuries holding exclusively to the lordship of Christ could cost someone their life when it translated into a refusal to burn incense before a statue of the Emperor, but in the Western world today the 'anything goes' attitude of post-modernism should ensure that Christians will not be persecuted, even though many will disagree with an exclusivist position. Indeed, it is more likely that the claims of Christians will be ignored as irrelevant rather than attacked. However, whether Christian claims to the uniqueness of Christ are attacked or ignored, they must be backed up by action if they are to be authenticated.

Christians in Ireland today can identify with the frustration of our message not really being understood. The church is often better known for what it is against rather than what it is for, while many people understand the Bible as emphasising what we should not do rather than outlining the new life that Christians know it offers.

Christians in Ireland can now be understood as being a bit 'weird'. Similarly, Christians in the pre-Constantinian period were usually viewed with great suspicion. Indeed, many inhabitants of the Roman Empire felt that Christians were atheists because they did not bow to statues and other tangible gods. Christians spoke of a god who could not be seen or touched in any tangible way and, therefore, this was no god at all. Rumours also abounded that Christians were cannibals because at their services they talked about eating Jesus' flesh and drinking his blood.

However, the tide was turned in the second and third centuries because, despite not understanding the theology, people increasingly saw that Christianity worked, that Christians cared for each other and for others and that the Christian lifestyle was a good one. In a context where an explanation of Christianity was suspect, a demonstration of Christianity was often persuasive.

Here are clear lessons for Christians in Ireland today. Our message is increasingly misunderstood or viewed with suspicion, if it is known at all. As in the early centuries, Christians today must demonstrate a lifestyle that is attractive enough to make people want to engage with their message.

Many missiologists and mission practitioners today speak of the need for the Church to be accessible, that it should be easy for people to drift into our services and feel immediately comfortable. Yet, in the Church of the second and third centuries, inviting friends and neighbours to worship was not part of their mission strategy. It could not be because newcomers were not allowed to come into the service without some prior catechesis. In these early centuries of the Church, by the time someone came to a worship service they knew exactly what they were getting into. People lived attractive lives in the community, but it was not easy to join the Church and newcomers had to undergo a lengthy process to become a member. Halter and Smay conclude that,

> "As you reflect on the values of the early Church, you'll notice that there's not much that reflects a 'seeker' orientation or a desire to pander to the dominant culture, either religious or pagan. No effort was put into making participation in the Christian community easy, fake, or personally beneficial".[22]

The rapid growth of Christianity in the first three centuries of the Church "happened through what seems now to us as rather introverted Christian communities".[23] The hurdle which had to be jumped by those who wanted to join the Church was quite high, but people were attracted to Christianity due to the lifestyle that they saw in the Christians.

Raymond Fung tells of a homeless lady with numerous health problems who often received assistance at an Episcopalian centre for homeless people in Kansas. As time went by she got to know the staff and she also began to realise that they were praying people. One day she asked if someone could pray for her and, as a result, she was invited to come and pray with them the next morning, which happened to be Good Friday. Someone read one of the Gospel accounts of the death of Jesus after which the homeless lady who was visiting spoke up, "If there are people like you in the world, perhaps Jesus really was raised from the dead".[24] The lifestyle and, in this case, social outreach of the Christians she encountered led her to begin to engage with their message.

There are lessons here for the Church today. Perhaps there needs to be less focus on making our worship services accessible and understandable. Christians must again catch outsiders' attention by their distinctive lifestyle. The key is authenticity. If Christian lifestyle is authentically different and distinctively better, then people will be attracted to Christianity. Furthermore, when they come they will recognise worship that is authentic and real whether or not they fully understand it and can engage with it at first,

"The key to authentic worship is the presence of authentic worshippers. They transform the most routine liturgies into encounters with the love and glory of God. Maybe our question should not be how to make worship more appealing to people outside of the Churches. But rather how should Christians worship together authentically".[25]

I am reminded of the words of a Presbyterian Minister who was sent to a small church in Kilkenny a few decades ago. The building was in bad repair and there was only a small group in the congregation. During his ministry, the congregation grew dramatically and new premises were built. From the beginning their prayer was that everyone who entered their musty old building would sense the presence of God there. "The cinema had more comfortable seats, the pub had better music but no-one else could offer the presence of God".[26]

GENTLE WORDS

So, authentic Christian lifestyle incarnated outside the church is the key to mission today. Yet presence alone is not enough – the name of Christ has to be spoken at some stage. As well as the demonstration of real Christianity there must always be some form of proclamation of Christ as Saviour. It has to be a combination of both "gospel proclaimed and gospel practiced".[27] As one of the New Testament Epistles puts it, Christians must "always be prepared to give an answer to everyone who asks you to give the reason for the hope that you have".[28] Given that these words are preceded by "in your hearts, set apart Christ as Lord", it seems that the picture being presented here is that, as Christians following Jesus are seen to be distinctly different, people will ask about the source of their particular way of living and more hopeful outlook on life.[29]

Following on from their net of friendship image (mentioned in Chapter Five) Frost and Hirsch continue,

"As the net is being repaired and tightened, not-yet-Christians are bound to come into contact with my evangelist friend. We believe that if our not-yet-Christian friends were swept into a series of friendships with a number of incarnational Christians, at least one of whom is an evangelist; God will do his work of bringing people into a relationship with him".[30]

I clearly saw this principle at work during my time in Kerry where there was one man in particular who had a God-given gift of getting alongside people who had come into the church and invariably ended up leading them to Christ in a most gentle but effective manner. He himself had experienced a life-changing conversion decades earlier and he was greatly used by God in connecting with people who had drifted into the church community for various reasons, but who ended up making a personal commitment to Jesus Christ.

I remember often being in a crowded room after a service, while coffee and buns were liberally distributed, and seeing this gentleman over in some corner gently meeting with a newcomer. It was a beautiful thing to watch because I knew that it was likely that somebody was going to discover the life-changing grace of Christ through the gentle sharing of a gifted evangelist.

Ephesians 4:11 provides a list of people in local churches who had particular gifts, "to prepare God's people for works of service, so the body of Christ may be built up".[31] Murray correctly observes that the fact that this list includes evangelists suggests that evangelists played a much more localised educational role in the Church rather than acting as "eloquent performers in public events".[32] So Croft argues, "The role of the evangelist is no longer to proclaim a summary of the gospel in the expectation that people would respond. The evangelist moves from the pulpit to the lounge /pub and becomes someone you can chat and laugh with".[33]

There is then a growing consensus amongst missiologists and Church leaders that evangelism is at its best when it takes place in the context of already established relationships. Bob Roxburgh who advocates Church as a cluster of small cells speaks for many.

> *"In our desire to reach our neighbourhood and people in our own spheres of influence with the gospel of Jesus Christ, we will discover that when all the different schemes are said and done it will be a small group of people living incarnate in their neighbourhood, practicing the gift of hospitality and living out the dynamic of the gospel that will have the most effective impact in the long term"*.[34]

In referring to 1 Peter 3:15 as I have done above, it is important not to leave out the last sentence of the verse. Just after urging people to be prepared to give an answer to everyone who asks, Peter cautions his readers, "But do this with gentleness and respect".[35] When Christ is being proclaimed the impact of what is said can be greatly reduced by *how* it is said. If Christians are to be good news, then they must be careful about how they speak to the world.

In particular, when Christians make pronouncements on moral issues, they often portray a lack of love so that people outside the Church simply do not believe Christians when they say that they love them.[36] Halter and Smay present a real challenge to the Church.

> *"Our main contention is that what drew people to Jesus, surprisingly, was not his message. It was him. His face, the softness in his voice, the whimsical look he gave the children, how he laughed, and how he lived. His message repelled people. Many people who were drawn to him as a man would leave after he had let them in on the message. This is quite a switch for most of us. We try to draw others by soft-pedalling the message and end up repelling them by how we live our lives"*.[37]

It is a question of order. If Christians speak first, then the words have little effect on those outside the Church and, indeed, may put people off their message. However, if people see something different in the way Christians live and then ask what the reason is, it gives those Christians the opportunity to verbalise their faith in a way that will get a hearing. Then, when we are offered a hearing, the way that we speak is crucial. As noted in Chapter One, the records of Paul's travels indicate that when he stopped in a place his ministry there was not necessarily high profile. It is probable that Paul spent much time with fellow tentmakers and other people in the marketplace. These times would have been dominated by one-to-one discussions or small groups talking together about the faith.

Furthermore, even when Paul was preaching, there is evidence that it was not a monologue. Acts often uses the Greek verb διαλέγομαι (*dialegomai*) when describing Paul's ministry in places such as Ephesus, Athens and Corinth. The use of this word implies a discussion rather than Paul preaching a sermon while people listened passively. It is particularly noteworthy that dialogue played a central part in Paul's preaching of the gospel because, during recent centuries of Church history in the Western world, evangelism has mostly been understood as simple proclamation of the truth.

In today's environment, when the idea of objective truth is increasingly under pressure, modern evangelism needs to incorporate an element of listening and dialogue, while at the same time communicating Christ. Christians often see Paul primarily as a great proclaimer/preacher of the gospel and indeed he was. But he also listened to people, gained an understanding of them and dialogued with them. As a result, his presentation of Christ was more relevant to them. In this regard Paul clearly seems to have lessons for the present-day evangelist.

CHRISTIAN CARING

As well as the Church's social outreach to others, caring relationships within the Church community can also act as an effective method of mission. In France, over 70 years ago, Godon and Daniel note that out of the hundreds of recent converts they questioned, "three quarters were captured through the friendliness of the little Christian groups they got among".[38] They assert that, for the mission of the Church to progress, Christian groups need to be relatively small and to portray a deep unity along with mutual compassion and care.[39]

Writing on the basis of his much more recent research into hundreds of growing churches around the world, Schwarz concurs. "Unfeigned, practical love has a divinely generated magnetic power far more effective than evangelistic programmes which depend almost entirely on verbal communication. People do not want to hear us talk about love; they want to experience how Christian love really works".[40] A few years ago we had a college student from France staying in our home who had virtually no knowledge of Christianity; when Christmas came she asked me to explain the figures in our nativity scene. But shortly after Christmas, one of our family had to spend some weeks in hospital and numerous people from the church delivered cooked meals to our door. Seeing this had a big impact on our student visitor, Christian caring in action.

Finney observes that Paul's letters say little about their duty to evangelise but a lot about their unity with each other. Paul "knew that in his day it was Christian common life that would attract attention and bring converts. This is still true".[41] The deep sense of fellowship and mutual caring within the Church which the New Testament advocates helped to make this new religion attractive to people in a harsh society. Also, the understanding that even slave and free are equal in Christ must have made a big impact. Evidence suggests that the early Church, at least partially, crossed over boundaries of class and income level, which were prevalent in the stratified society of the Roman Empire. This may mean that the early Church has lessons to teach the Church of today in that divisions of class and social standing are now tending to break down.

Here in Ireland, as in most other countries in the Western world, class boundaries were well defined and generally accepted by everyone. There was a sense that people knew their place and that society functioned better if everyone stayed in their place. However, thankfully that has now changed and, in general, people are impressed when they see groups and organisations which treat everyone the same and where distinctions of class, social position or economic standing are not enforced. For Christians, everyone who is a child of God is, by definition, of equal status because all are children of the same Father.

The early Church was clear on this truth and leaders like Paul were quick to speak out if the church drifted into class divisions. So too, mission in Ireland today will benefit if the church holds fast to this principle. We call ourselves 'Ireland of the welcomes' but we do not have to dig too far below the surface to realise that Ireland has its fair share of racism and ethnic intolerance. Yet, if the church can really model what it looks like to be a unified community transcending social, cultural, ethnic or any other division, then it will make our witness much more attractive.

In the second and third centuries the community life of the Church continued to have an impact. Christians conveyed to the wider society that they cared deeply for each other.

"It was not as a disembodied truth uttered into the air that the Christian good news laid hold of men: it was through the corporate life of the little Christian societies in the cities of the ancient world. [Anyone] coming into contact with such a group felt an atmosphere unlike anything else".[42]

It was common in Roman society for people to find themselves living in a city where they had no family links. In this environment, where isolated and lonely people looked for community, the caring family atmosphere of the church could prove very attractive. This too is something for the church in Ireland to bear in mind. A generation or two ago, most Irish people lived in the place where they had grown up, but increasingly this is not the case. Furthermore, in recent decades, Ireland has become a place to which people have come to live from all over the world. If the church can demonstrate itself to be a loving community of mutual care, it can appeal to people feeling isolated and far from home.

The congregation which I currently pastor has been blessed by the fact that many people have joined us in recent years having moved to Ireland from around the world. Many of them would say that the congregation has become their Irish family, helping them to cope with being far away from relatives at home.

As discussed in Chapter Two, Christian caring was often expressed by covering the funeral expenses of church members whose family could not afford it. This was one of the ways that the fellowship of the church could attract people to Christianity. I too have seen the care of a congregation for one of their number who has had a bereavement becoming a powerful witness to other friends and family members who were not Christians.

OFFERING HOPE

At a meeting of representatives from various Methodist Churches around the world in June 2021, I heard the Leader of the Church in Portugal describe how, when Covid restrictions closed their buildings, they were worried that it would "take church off everyone's radar. But actually, the opposite is true because Church members *got out* to serve the community".[43] As well as living amongst people, making friendships and speaking about Christ when asked, Christians also need to be watchful for practical ways to help people who are outside the Church. This remains a key way to make an impact for Christ amongst non-Christian people.

Chuck Colson points out that when the Communist party took over Russia in 1917 they did not make Christianity illegal, but they made it illegal for the Church to do any good works such as feeding the hungry, housing orphans, educating children or caring for the sick. As a result, within a few decades the Church was irrelevant to the communities in which it was placed. Hence, "Take away service and you take away the Church's power, influence, and evangelistic effectiveness. The power of the gospel is combining the life-changing message with selfless service".[44]

To quote Frost and Hirsch again, while "relationships are being built, Christian believers should be demonstrating a holy lifestyle through acts of generosity and kindness, by a preference for the poor and suffering, and by a love for the scorned".[45] The bottom line is that if someone comes into contact with a Christian, it should be good news for them. The fact that someone is a Christian should benefit those around them.

As we have seen, during the second and third centuries, Christian care was often expressed in helping the poor, feeding prisoners, caring for the sick and supporting the bereaved. There is also evidence that such social care stretched beyond the Church circle into the wider community. This certainly had an impact and would have attracted many to Christianity. Here in Ireland, there was a time when the Church provided most of the healthcare and education but, now that these are largely taken care of by the State, we do well to ask ourselves what are the current social needs of people around us and what can we do to help meet them? As Michael Frost puts it, "a core question for all missional Christians is to ask, what does the reign of God through Christ look like in my neighbourhood?...This is a far more legitimate and creative question than the usual questions about how we can attract people to our church programs".[46]

After the conversion of Constantine, the Church's social work often came to be organised on an institutional scale and funding from the Imperial authorities began to be channelled into Church-run hospitals, food distribution centres and orphanages. Consequently, while social outreach work increased, its effectiveness as a means for influencing people towards conversion to Christianity was reduced as direct links with Christian congregations were diluted.

Written in the 1970s Vincent Donovan's account of his work amongst the Masai People in Tanzania has become a seminal study on Christian mission. Early in the book Donovan records one of his first conversations with an influential Masai elder called Ndangoay. Donovan records that he,

"Pointed out that we were well known among the Masai for our work in schools and hospitals, and for our interest in the Masai and their cattle. But now I no longer wanted to talk about schools and hospitals, but about God in the life of the Masai, and about the message of Christianity. Indeed, it was for this very work of explaining the message of Christianity to the different peoples of Africa that I came here from far away. Ndangoay

looked at me for a long time, and then said in a puzzled way, 'If that is why you came here, why did you wait so long to tell us about this?'[47]

Donovan admits that he had no answer to this question and it certainly highlights what can happen when the link is lost between Christian-initiated social outreach and the Christian community that initiated it. Instances of this danger are easy to see in Ireland. For example, the "Bons Secours" hospitals, which began as Christian missions are now expensive hospitals where only those with private health insurance can go. Some years ago, in a conversation with the Superintendent Minister of the Leeds City Mission of the Methodist Church in Britain, I was told that, although the Mission executes many fine social programmes, the impact for Christ on the city is limited because few of the beneficiaries are aware of its Christian raison d'être. I have come to understand this issue better since being appointed as the Methodist Minister in charge of Dublin Central Mission.

The Mission goes back well over a hundred years and, as the name suggests, has always been attached to a church building and its congregation in the city centre (initially George's Street and more recently Lower Abbey Street). For at least the first half of its existence, the Mission's work was almost entirely amongst people in the heart of Dublin city and mostly involved assisting people with basic material needs such as heating fuel, food vouchers and such like.

Then, in the 1950s the Mission opened the first sheltered housing colony (as it was called then) for older people in Ireland. This was in response to a growing awareness of the unacceptable living conditions of people who had reached retirement age. Over time this work grew and now Dublin Central Mission runs two sheltered housing complexes and a nursing home providing residence and care for over 130 older people. These centres are located in the suburbs of Sandymount and Glenageary while there is still a Mission Centre in Abbey Street.

The Abbey Street building houses a church congregation, hosts many different addiction support groups, offers English conversation classes to vulnerable migrant peoples who cannot afford commercial schools of English and holds various 'open-doors' gatherings for people who are lonely or want company with others. It is also a base from which small groups go out to offer food, clothes and conversation to people who are homeless.

However, while some of the core of the original work of the Mission continues in Abbey Street, there is always the danger that 'the tail ends up wagging the dog' in that most of the budget and staff is focused on the centres for care of older people. That is not to say that this is a bad thing, but there needs to be constant awareness of the danger that the ethos which drives the Mission could be lost. It is all too easy for a resident or staff member in any of our centres to be unaware of the rest of the Mission's work and of the motivating reason which drives what we do.

Stephen Skuce offers this challenge, "the calling on the Church today is to be primarily a community of faith. Christians need to be noted as spiritual people who care for others rather than community minded people who are also religious".[48] In the recent past, and as a culmination of the direction of travel which began after Constantine, the Church, not least in Ireland, became the main institutional provider of health-care and education. Now that these institutions are largely funded and administered by the State, the Church can have "liberty to recognise its chief calling as a spiritual community rather than as a handmaiden to the state".[49]

That is not to say that the Church should have no role in healthcare and education. But there is now an opportunity to ensure that Church involvement is specifically targeted at gaps in State provision rather than just being part of it. This means that the Church can focus on those who are most excluded from or disadvantaged by the State systems.

We have seen how monks began to facilitate social outreach work in their neighbourhoods. No doubt some of the beneficiaries were influenced towards conversion to Christianity. For example, a visit to the ruins at Clonmacnoise on the banks of the River Shannon makes it easy to imagine the impact such a community must have had on the people of the surrounding area. Of particular note are the monastic communities established on mainland Europe by Columbanus and his followers. In what were largely barbarian cultures, each of these monastic settlements offered an oasis of hope through caring for the sick, educating children and propagating improved agricultural techniques. They brought blessing to their community and showed people that life could be better. These monks of old bring a challenge to Christians in Ireland – how can we find ways of showing people a positive alternative?

Regarding the travels of Irish monks, Lehane concludes that, "Wherever they went the Irish retained their personality and stayed outside the mainstream. Many responded to their sincerity and fundamentalism and the slightly mystical aura that always surrounded them".[50]

In post-modern Ireland people will not necessarily warm to the Christian message or even understand it, while substantial numbers of people in Ireland today view the Church as part of the problem. Christians need to find ways of showing that living as a Christian is better – that Jesus really did mean it when He said that he had come that we might have "life in all its fullness".[51] Even before we talk about our faith, let us and our congregations become known as oases of hope showing a positive alternative in our cities, towns and rural areas.

In discussing this I find my mind going back 30 years to an isolated rural village in Haiti called Dory. There is a Methodist church building in Dory, packed with people praising God. Then, at the side of the church is the primary school, behind that is the health centre, across the way is the water pump with an agriculture project behind and in front of that is the community shop. The church also runs a truck, which drives through the river to the road and on to a large town so people can sell their produce at the market. Written in big letters on the front of the truck is the French word 'Espoir' meaning 'Hope'.

If we went to Dory and did a survey asking people, 'Does it affect you that that church is there?' you can guess what the answer would be. But what would the answer be if the same survey was done here and the question was asked about our church? Of course the needs of Dory are different to the needs we are likely to encounter where our churches are placed here in Ireland, but do we know what the needs are in our local community and are we looking for ways to address them in Jesus' name? Do people who live and work near our churches benefit from the fact that our congregation meets there?

In the synagogue at Nazareth, Jesus chose words from Isaiah to describe his mission.

> "The Spirit of the Lord is on me, because he has anointed me to proclaim good news to the poor. He has sent me to proclaim freedom for the prisoners and recovery of sight for the blind, to set the oppressed free, to proclaim the year of the Lord's favour".[52]

Dallas Willard points out that this good news sounds this-worldly as well as spiritual.[53] Christians are not only called to tell others about Christ, we are called to offer better life to others in Christ's name. Yet, in a recent survey only 8% of non-Christian, Irish young people agreed with a statement that "most people of faith are good for Ireland".[54] This is tragic and presents an urgent challenge to the church.

STRATEGY?

In Psalm 105:12-13 we read, "God's people were few in number, strangers in the land of Canaan. They wandered from country to country, from one kingdom to another".[55] Although these verses refer to the people of Israel in the Old Testament, they also describe the countless people through whom the message of Christ arrived in places far beyond the Roman Empire, as discussed in Chapter Four. Long before Ulfilas crossed the Rhine many Germanic barbarians had been influenced towards Christianity by the faithful witness of ordinary people. Some of these had been carried from the Empire as captives and must have suffered horribly. Nevertheless, their Christian lifestyle had an impact. In addition, Christian merchants and other travellers often played a part in the dissemination of the Christian message. Countless unnamed individuals who travelled in every direction beyond the political boundaries of the Roman Empire taking their Christianity with them.

Long before Patrick, Christianity entered Ireland through trade links with Southern Wales. The most common way in which the news of Jesus Christ spread was through ordinary people – merchants, slaves and other travellers. Yet, Christianity was generally not the reason why these folk travelled but, because they were Christians, when they travelled the Christian message travelled with them. They ended up as missionaries sharing Jesus wherever they went.

There is an important lesson in this for us today. Mission need not be something that we necessarily do intentionally. Mission should not be one activity in our lives that we maybe engage in on a certain night of the week. Rather mission is about following God in our lives, growing closer in our relationship with Him and, as we do so, then we end up sharing Him with others.

The follow on from this is that mission need not be something we feel pressured to do. As Christians our ultimate calling is to be Christians, that is to be people who walk in relationship with Jesus Christ, who follow him and who seek to grow closer to Him each day. If that is our primary aim then mission will happen.

Real mission is at its best when it is unforced, when it is a product of a person's daily walk with Jesus, when it happens because someone asks God to reveal to them where He is working in their circumstances and to guide them as to how they can join in with what He is doing.

It is debatable whether the Church in the first three centuries ever really had a mission strategy. In place of evidence of strategy and planning for mission in the New Testament era, the overall sense is that the early Christians followed God and went where they saw the Spirit moving. In the early years of my ordained ministry (late 1990s) I remember hearing talks and reading books which challenged me to have a five-year plan for the church. I clearly remember during those days feeling inadequate and a bit guilty because I really did not have a plan. I was passionate about mission, I firmly believed that Jesus was the answer to people's needs and that we had good news to share. I further believed that God could and would work through the local churches for which I was responsible, but I really did not have any sort of road map.

Over 20 years later I still have no five-year plan, but I no longer feel bad about it because I have learned that my responsibility is to watch for where, as the old song puts it, "I hear the sound of rustling in the leaves of the trees".[56]

What was true during the early Christian centuries remains equally true today – God is at work and our calling is to watch for what God is doing and get on board. Mission is less what we initiate and more what we join in with – God is the Initiator and He invites us to follow – to tailgate the God of Mission.[57]

New Testament Christians clearly exhibited a passion for mission and a desire to tell others about Jesus, but, certainly in the early years, this seems to have been an unplanned, spontaneous movement. It appears that, as peoples' lives were changed, it resulted in them developing a desire to tell others of Jesus wherever they found themselves. The Apostle Paul spoke for many of his contemporaries when he wrote that "Christ's love compels us".[58] The French translation of that verse is used as the motto of the Methodist Church in Haiti. So, on the walls of many church buildings there you will see a crest which includes the words, "L'amour du Christ nous possede". This translates as 'the love of Christ possesses us'.

In the New Testament we see that principle at work. When people meet God they become possessed with the desire to tell others. Some years ago I had that conversation with a judge in Dublin during an Asylum Hearing. I was speaking on behalf of a young man who belonged to the congregation I pastored at the time. He had come from Iran where he had recently converted to Christianity, which put his life in danger. The point at issue in the Hearing was whether his conversion was genuine. If it was he would be granted refugee status but it had to be proved that he was not just saying he was converted to Christianity so he could live in Ireland.

One of the arguments the Irish State was using to say that perhaps his conversion was not genuine, was the fact that he was active in witnessing to others. They said that surely such a new Christian would not be so confident to share their faith. I informed the judge that, in my experience, the exact opposite is usually true. When somebody meets Jesus personally it is such a wonderful life-changing experience that they want to tell others. In fact, sometimes it is people who have been Christians for longer that can forget the wonder of it all and be less inclined to share their faith.

Thankfully, my friend got his refugee status in Ireland. But the point is, meeting with Jesus leads us to want to share Jesus. The Christians of the New Testament did not engage in mission because they were commanded to. It was because they discovered good news and wanted to share it.

If something good happens in your life you will rush home to tell someone and it will not be long until you have it up on social media. I remember the morning after our first child was born I was walking past the Longford shopping centre and I suddenly thought that I would like to climb up on the roof and announce the news. We love to share good news, so if you do not want to share then maybe it's because there is no fresh good news and you need to meet Jesus again?

CONCLUSION

During the first three Christian centuries we see mission and church growth from a place of pressure. During these days of declining numbers in many Christian Churches around Ireland, there can be the temptation to feel that the focus must be on preserving the church, battening down the hatches and ensuring our survival. For some this tendency increased during the recent Covid pandemic. No in-person services, reduced offerings and an uncertain future caused some individual Christians and even whole congregations to feel that they had enough on their plate without having to think about mission or outreach. But why should this be?

To ask oneself, 'what is God doing in this situation and how can I get on board with Him in His mission?' is an invigorating, enlivening question, which can actually relieve pressure rather than cause it.

Before Constantine, we saw a church which was under real pressure from society and sometimes from the authorities as well. However, although it often had to meet in secret, this church remained outward facing through the individual lifestyle of each member. In times of uncertainty and difficulty they offered real hope and tangible social care even to people who misunderstood them. This is how the church grew during its first three centuries, this is how the church can grow today.

Conclusion

Hope from the Margins

The margins can be an uncomfortable place and the Church in the Western world is feeling that more and more. This brings to an end a long period of comfort, which started after Constantine. But this period of comfort was also a time when the Church tended to become shallow and lose its distinctiveness. Then there was coercion, where the Church made people feel uncomfortable (or worse) if they were outside of it. So too, in recent Irish history, the Church has left a bitter taste for some and driven many away.

But now, from our place of discomfort in the margins, we have an opportunity to share our message differently following the example of Christians during the earliest centuries of the Church who rarely felt comfortable, yet tended to be stronger in faith and more effective in mission.

"The Word became flesh and made his dwelling among us" is one of the best-known verses in the Bible and it concisely summarises God's mission to the world by Incarnation – God sent, Jesus came.[1] But when the Word became flesh, He went to the margins. He did not make His dwelling in Rome or any other great city, but in mostly rural areas of an obscure province in the far east of the Empire. He spent much more time with marginalised people than with the rich and powerful.

Incarnation has recently been beautifully described as "the body language of God".[2] By coming to this world, the incarnate Christ gave up power and comfort, telling His followers, "I am among you as one who serves".[3] With a servant posture Jesus brought hope to the world from the margins. So, what about His Church?

During the first three centuries after Jesus' ascension the fledgling Church largely continued to hold a servant posture. It served people and offered hope. Those who encountered Christians saw something authentically different and good. They were attracted to the early Church by the quality of the Christians' lifestyles even though they were culturally different to those around them.

But after Constantine, the Church grew in numbers, power and influence, quickly becoming a ruling authority, dominating culture. As State and Church grew together, so their values and culture merged and much of the distinctiveness of Christianity was lost. Now, as a former Bishop of Southwark put it, "We have moved from where Christianity is culture to where Christianity is choice".[4]

The Church is at the margins now. We are no longer central to society. That leaves us with a choice. We can slowly die in marginal irrelevance, or we can offer hope from the margins. We can sit in the margins praying and hoping that someday 'they will come', or we can live authentically distinctive lives wherever we are; caring, welcoming, gently speaking in ways that make people wonder why we are different. This is what Jesus did when he walked the earth. This is how his followers lived in the early centuries even though they were marginalised. This is what we can choose to do today.

We are in the margins. We have a choice. What will you and your church choose? The Church has lost its position of power and privilege. But that gives us the opportunity to better follow our Master who "made himself nothing by taking the very nature of a servant".[5] In this way Christ made salvation available to all the world. Following Him, and empowered by His Spirit, we can joyfully share His message of hope, from the margins.

Endnotes

INTRODUCTION
1 Lynda Neilands "The Methodist Newsletter", Vol. 41, No 442, May 2013, p2.
2 Acts 2:41. Unless otherwise indicated all Bible quotations are taken from the Holy Bible, New International Version - Anglicised Edition. (1984).
3 Matthew 6:28.
4 Christian Schwarz, *Natural Church Development*, p11.
5 Herbert Butterfield, *Christianity and History*, p135.

CHAPTER 1
1 Acts 1:8.
2 John Drane, *Evangelism for a New Age*, p74-76.
3 James Fleming, "Acts: New Discoveries from the Early Church", Lecture on cassette produced by Biblical Resources, Jerusalem.
4 Romans 15:24,28. Note also that 1 Clement 5 describes Paul as having travelled "to the extreme limit of the west" which some interpret as Spain or even Britain.
5 Acts 1:12.
6 Acts 2:6.
7 Acts 2:41.
8 Acts 2:42-47.
9 Acts 3.
10 Acts 4:29-30.
11 Acts 5:17-18.
12 Acts 5:20.
13 Acts 5:42.
14 Acts 5:28.
15 Acts 5:29-32.
16 Acts 4:20.
17 David Peterson, *The Acts of the Apostles*, p215.
18 Acts 6:4.
19 Peterson, *The Acts of the Apostles*, p229. See Acts 5:42; 6:7; 12:24; 19:20.
20 Acts 8:4.

21 Craig Keener, *Bible Background Commentary: New Testament*, (Comment on John 10:23 where Jesus is recorded as walking in Solomon's Colonnade), p291.
22 For example, the parable of the Great Banquet in Luke 14:15-23.
23 For example, Matthew 9:10-11.
24 Santos Yao, "Dismantling Social Barriers Through Table Fellowship", p33. Found in Robert Gallagher & Paul Hertig (eds.), *Mission in Acts*, p29-36.
25 Acts 9:36.
26 Acts 9:39.
27 Lewis Foster, "The Chronology and Metrology of the New Testament". Found in *The Expositor's Bible Commentary*. Vol. 8, p600.
28 Acts 11:26. See Norman Thomas, "The Church at Antioch: Crossing Racial, Cultural, and Class Barriers", p153. Found in Gallagher & Hertig (eds.), *Mission in Acts*, p29-36.
29 Peterson, *The Acts of the Apostles*, p374.
30 William Larkin, *Acts,* p190.
31 Acts 13:12.
32 Acts 13:14-48.
33 Acts 14:1&3.
34 Acts 19:17-20.
35 Acts 19:20.
36 Acts 26:16.
37 1 Corinthians 9:16.
38 Acts 14:21-23.
39 Romans 15:19,23.
40 Walter Taylor, *Paul, Apostle to the Nations*, p92.
41 1 Thessalonians 1:8c.
42 Wayne Meeks, *The First Urban Christians,* p27.
43 Paul probably arrived in Corinth around 49 AD. See Alan Cole, "The Life and Ministry of Paul," Found in *The Expositor's Bible Commentary*. Vol 8.p572. The two periods of ministry (one of two years and one of three months) in Ephesus were during the years 54-57 AD. Lewis Foster, "The Chronology and Metrology of the New Testament". Found in *The Expositor's Bible Commentary*. Vol. 8, p601.
44 Fleming, "Acts: New Discoveries from the Early Church". Lecture on cassette produced by Biblical Resources, Jerusalem.
45 Fleming, "Acts: New Discoveries from the Early Church".
46 Acts 28:1-10.
47 Acts 19:37.
48 Fleming, "Acts: New Discoveries from the Early Church".
49 1 Corinthians 9:22.
50 Acts 19:9.
51 Acts 17:17.
52 Acts 18:4.
53 Acts 14:7 & 17:15-34.

Endnotes

54 Acts 18:1-3.
55 Meeks, *The First Urban Christians*, p29.
56 Ronald Hock, *The Social Context of Paul's Ministry*, p41.
57 Taylor, *Paul, Apostle to the Nations*, p100.
58 1 Corinthians 6:9-11.
59 For example, Frederick Bruce, *The Spreading Flame*, p118.
60 Origen, *Against Celsus*, 3.59.
61 1 Corinthians 7:20-24 & Ephesians 6:5-8.
62 Richard Bauckham, *The Book of Acts in its Palestinian Setting*, p218.
63 Acts 16:14.
64 Fleming, "Acts: New Discoveries from the Early Church". Lecture on cassette produced by Biblical Resources, Jerusalem.
65 Acts 13:4-12.
66 Michael Green, *Evangelism in the Early Church*, p317.
67 Eckhard Schnabel, *Paul the Missionary*, p337.
68 Green, *Evangelism in the Early Church*, p141.
69 Schnabel, *Paul the Missionary*, p357.
70 Acts 2:46 & 5:42.
71 Acts 12:12.
72 Acts 10:22-48 & 16:32.
73 Acts 18:26.
74 Acts 18:1-4.
75 Green, *Evangelism in the Early Church*, p252.
76 Green, *Evangelism in the Early Church*, p253.
77 William Lane, "Social Prospectus on Roman Christianity during the formative years from Nero to Nerva: Romans, Hebrews, 1 Clement". p208. Found in Karl Donfried and Peter Richardson, *Judaism and Christianity in 1st Century Rome*, p196 – 244.
78 Bruce Frier, *Landlords and Tenants in Imperial Rome*. Cited by Schnabel, *Paul the Missionary*, p300.
79 Taylor, *Paul, Apostle to the Nations*, p95.
80 1 Corinthians 14:23.
81 Lane, "Social Prospectus on Roman Christianity during the formative years from Nero to Nerva: Romans, Hebrews, 1 Clement", p209. Found in Donfried & Richardson, *Judaism and Christianity in 1st Century Rome*, p196 – 244.
82 1 Thessalonians 4:12.
83 1 Peter 2:9.
84 1 Peter 2:12.
85 1 Peter 2:15.
86 1 Corinthians 5:10.
87 1 Corinthians 7:12-16.
88 1 Corinthians 10:33.
89 1 Corinthians 14:23-25.

90 Craig de Vos, "Popular Graeco-Roman Responses to Christianity" p870. Found in Philip Esler, *The Early Christian World*. Vol. 2, p869-889.
91 De Vos, "Popular Graeco-Roman Responses to Christianity" p870-1. Found in Esler, *The Early Christian World*. Vol. 2, p869-889.
92 1 Peter 1:14.

CHAPTER 2
1 Note that the term "missionary" in this section need not imply travel to another place but simply an involvement in the mission/outreach/evangelism of the Church.
2 Eusebius, *Ecclesiastical History*, 3.37.
3 Origen, *Against Celsus*, 3.52.
4 Origen, *Against Celsus*, 3.9.
5 Sozomen, *Ecclesiastical History*, 2.
6 *Didaché*, 11 & 12.
7 Ramsey MacMullen, *Christianizing the Roman Empire*, p34.
8 Luke 10:7.
9 *Didaché*, 11.
10 Johannes Weiss, *Earliest Christianity*, p680.
11 Minucius Felix, *Octavius*, 8.4.
12 Alan Kreider, *The Change of Conversion and the Origin of Christendom*, p11.
13 Ignatius, *Letter to Polycarp*, 1.
14 *The Martyrdom of Polycarp*, 12.
15 Irenaeus, *Against Heresies*, Book 1, Preface 3.
16 Gregory of Nyssa, *Life of Gregory Thaumatorgus*, J.53.
17 Gregory of Nyssa, *Life of Gregory Thaumatorgus*, J.53.
18 Kenneth Latourette, *The First Five Centuries*, p89.
19 David Bosch, *Transforming Mission*, p201.
20 Bosch, *Transforming Mission*, p201.
21 Polycarp, *Epistle to the Philippians*, 10.
22 Latourette, *The First Five Centuries*, p116.
23 Acts 19:9.
24 M. Smith, "Spreading the Good News". Found in *Lion Handbook of Christianity*, p86.
25 Dale Irvin & Scott Sunquist, *History of the World Christian Movement*, p89.
26 Origen, *Against Celsus*, 3.54.
27 Jean Danièlou, *Gospel Message and Hellenistic Culture*, p9.
28 Aristides, *Apology*, 16.5.
29 Dimitris Kayertatas, "The Significance of Leadership and Organization in the Spread of Christianity". Found in William Harris (ed.), *The Spread of Christianity in the First Four Centuries*, p55.
30 Kreider, *The Change of Conversion and the Origin of Christendom*, p16.
31 Eusebius, *Ecclesiastical History*, 8.12.

Endnotes

32 Justin, *Dialogue with Trypho*, 110.
33 Tertullian, *Apology*, 50.
34 Tertullian, *Apology*, 50.
35 Lactantius, *Divine Institutes*, 23.
36 Justin, *Second Apology*, 12.
37 Eusebius, *Ecclesiastical History*, 6.5.
38 *Martyrdom of Perpetua*, 9.1.
39 *Martyrdom of Perpetua*, 16.4.
40 Tertullian, *Apology*, 50.
41 Marcus Aurelius, *Meditations*, 11.3.
42 Cited by Ramsey MacMullen, *Christianizing the Roman Empire*, p134, footnote 14.
43 W. Rordorf, "Martyr-Martyrdom" p531. Found in Berardino, *Encyclopaedia of the Early Church*, p531-532.
44 Basil of Caesarea, *Letter* 164, *To Ascholius*, 1.
45 For example, Elizabeth Clark, Duke University. http://www.pbs.org/wgbh/pages/frontline/shows/religion/why/martyrs.html#perpetua
46 Wolfgang Wischmeyer "The Sociology of Pre-Constantine Christianity: Approach from the Visible". Found in Alan Kreider, (ed.). *The Origins of Christendom in the West*, p149-151.
47 Eusebius, *Ecclesiastical History*, 8.1.
48 Eusebius, *Ecclesiastical History*, 8.1.
49 Vivian Green, *A New History of Christianity*, p20.
50 *Aboda Zarah*, Folio 27b.
51 Justin, *Second Apology*, 8.
52 Origen, *Against Celsus*, 1.46.
53 Cyprian, *To Demetrian*, 15.
54 Irenaeus, *Against Heresies*, 2.32.4. Italics mine.
55 *Gallagher*, "Conversion and Salvation in the Apocryphal Acts of the Apostles," *Journal of Early Christian Studies*. Vol. 8 *(1991)*. p4.
56 Eugene Gallagher, "Conversion and Salvation in the Apocryphal Acts of the Apostles," *Journal of Early Christian Studies*, Vol. 8 (1991), p4.
57 Gregory of Nyssa, *Life of Gregory Thaumaturgus*, J 27.
58 Gregory of Nyssa, *Life of Gregory Thaumaturgus*, J 28.
59 Gregory of Nyssa, *Life of Gregory Thaumaturgus*, J 43.
60 Origen, *Against Celsus*, 1.68.
61 Origen, *Against Celsus*, 1.68.
62 Origen, *Against Celsus*, 1.68.
63 Origen, *Against Celsus*, 1.68.
64 Michael Green, *Evangelism in the Early Church*, p227.
65 Remus, "Miracle", p753-754. Found in Everett Ferguson, *Encyclopaedia of Early Christianity*, p753-758.
66 Origen, *Against Celsus*, 3.24.
67 MacMullen, *Christianizing the Roman Empire*, p1.
68 Tertullian, *Apology*, 42.

69 Green, *Evangelism in the Early Church*, p12.
70 Bruce Winter, *Seek the Welfare of the City*, p209.
71 Glenn Hinson, *Early Christianity*, p70.
72 Athenagoras, *Embassy for the Christians*, 11.
73 Frederick Bruce, *The Spreading Flame*, p182.
74 *Martyrdom of St. Fructuoso.*
75 *Martyrdom of Polycarp*, 12.
76 Cited without reference by Vivian Green, *A New History of Christianity*, p23.
77 Origen, *Against Celsus*, 1.43.
78 Justin, *First Apology*, 7.
79 Justin, *Second Apology*, 2.
80 Minucius Felix, *Octavius*, 35.
81 Introduction to the Letter to Donatus in *The Fathers of the Church*, Vol. 36 (1958), p5.
82 Cyprian, *To Donatus*, 3.
83 *2 Clement*, 13.4. Cited by Kreider, *The Change of Conversion and the Origin of Christendom*, p18.
84 Justin, *First Apology*, 16.
85 Origen, *Against Celsus*, 7.49.
86 Translated by Edwyn Bevan, *Christianity*, p56. This passage from Galen is only preserved in an Arabic translation.
87 William Frend, *The Rise of Christianity*, p180.
88 Cited by Glenn Hinson, *The Evangelization of the Roman Empire*, p239-240.
89 *Didaché*, 1.1-2.
90 Justin, *First Apology*, 15-17.
91 *Epistle of Barnabas*, 21.
92 Clement, *First Epistle*, 33.
93 Ignatius, *Epistle to the Trallians*, 8.
94 Kreider, *The Change of Conversion and the Origin of Christendom*, p22.
95 *Apostolic Tradition*, 20.
96 Kreider, *The Change of Conversion and the Origin of Christendom*, p26. Italics mine.
97 *Apostolic Tradition*, 21.
98 Origen, *Against Celsus*, 3.55.
99 Latourette, *The First Five Centuries*, p117.
100 Josephus, *Against Apion*, 2.80.
101 Tertullian, *Ad Nationes*, 1:11 and Minucius Felix, *Octavius*, 9.
102 Oliver Yarbrough, "The Shadow of an Ass. On reading the Alexamenos Graffito". Found in Aliou Cissé Niang and Carolyn Osiek, Text, Image, and Christians in the Graeco-Roman World, p251.
103 Christopher Bryan, *The Resurrection of the Messiah*, p71.
104 Latourette, *The First Five Centuries*, p117.
105 Latourette, *The First Five Centuries*, p117.

Endnotes

106 Latourette, *The First Five Centuries*, p117.
107 Mark Humphries, *Early Christianity*, p119.
108 Latourette, *The First Five Centuries*, p117.
109 Stephen Neill, *A History of Christian Missions*, p41.
110 *Address to the Greeks*. Cited by Eberhard Arnold, *The Early Christians After the Death of the Apostles*, p88.
111 *Martyrdom of the Holy Martyrs: Justin, Chariton, Charites, Paeon, and Liberianus, who Suffered at Rome*, 3.
112 *Martyrdom of Perpetua*, 2.1; 20.6; 20.7.
113 Robert Wilken, *The Christians as the Romans saw them*, p35-6.
114 Tertullian, *Apology*, 39.
115 Green, *Evangelism in the Early Church*, p221.
116 Minucius Felix, *Octavius*, 9.
117 Rodney Stark, *The Rise of Christianity*, p156.
118 Stark, *The Rise of Christianity*, p158.
119 Raymond Brown, *The Churches the Apostles Left Behind*, p48.
120 *Epistle to Diognetus*, 10.6.
121 *Shepherd of Hermas*, Book 2. Commandment 8.10.
122 Justin, *First Apology*, 67.
123 Eusebius, *Ecclesiastical History*, 6.43.
124 Wolfgang Wischmeyer, "The Sociology of Pre-Constantine Christianity: approach from the visible". Found in Kreider (ed.), *The Origins of Christendom in the West*, p135.
125 Wischmeyer, "The Sociology of Pre-Constantine Christianity: approach from the visible". Found in Kreider (ed.), *The Origins of Christendom in the West*, p136.
126 Polycarp, *Epistle to the Philippians*, 6.
127 Pontius, *The Life and Passion of Cyprian*, 2.
128 Pontius, *The Life and Passion of Cyprian*, 3.
129 William Slater, "Handouts at Dinner". *Phoenix*, 54, p107-122.
130 Henry Chadwick, *The Church in Ancient Society*, p136.
131 Adolf Harnack, *The Expansion of Christianity in the First Three Centuries*, Vol. 1, p200.
132 Eusebius, *Ecclesiastical History*, 10.8.
133 Harnack, *The Expansion of Christianity in the First Three Centuries*, Vol. 1, p204.
134 Lucian, *The Passing of Peregrinus*, 12.
135 Lactantius, *Institutes*, 6.12.
136 Tertullian, *Apology*, 42.
137 Adolf Harnack, *The Expansion of Christianity in the First Three Centuries*, Vol. 1, p207.
138 *Canons of Hippolytus*, 24.199. Cited by Durell, *The Historic Church*, p286.
139 *Canons of Hippolytus*, 9.59.
140 Harnack, *The Expansion of Christianity in the First Three Centuries*, Vol.1, p150.

141 *Pseudo Justin,* 100.17. Cited by Harnack, *The Expansion of Christianity in the First Three Centuries,* Vol.1, p150.
142 Tertullian, *Letter to his Wife,* 2.4.
143 v12. "Live such good lives among the pagans that, though they accuse you of doing wrong, they may see your good deeds and glorify God on the day he visits us".
v15 "For it is God's will that by doing good you should silence the ignorant talk of foolish men".
144 Justin, *First Apology,* 62.
145 Pontius, *Life and Passion of Cyprian,* 9.
146 First Greek, *Life of Pachomius,* 4.
147 Eusebius, *Ecclesiastical History,* 4.23. This is rather reminiscent of the collection which the apostle Paul organised amongst the Gentile Churches to help the Christians in Jerusalem.
148 Eusebius, *Ecclesiastical History,* 7.22.
149 Eusebius, *Ecclesiastical History,* 7.22.
150 Eusebius, *Ecclesiastical History,* 9.8.
151 Pontius, *Life and Passion of Cyprian,* 9.
152 Justin Martyr, *First Apology,* 62.
153 *Didaché,* 1.5.
154 *Epistle of Barnabas,* 19.11.
155 Matthew 5:42.
156 Clement, *Second Epistle,* 16,
157 Cyprian, *On Works and Alms,* 24.
158 Wischmeyer, "The Sociology of Pre-Constantine Christianity: approach from the visible". Found in Kreider (ed.), *The Origins of Christendom in the West,* p148.
159 Stark, *The Rise of Christianity,* Chapter 7, p147-162.
160 Stark, *The Rise of Christianity,* p154.
161 Stark, *The Rise of Christianity,* p149.
162 Hinson, *Early Christianity,* p63.
163 Julian the Apostate, *Letters,* 22. *To Arsacius.*

CHAPTER 3
1 Robert Markus, *Christianity in the Roman World,* p107.
2 Adam Serfass, A. "Wine for Widows" p89-90. Found in Susan Holman, *Wealth and Poverty in Early Church and Society,* p88-102.
3 CTh 5.73. Cited by Henry Chadwick, *The Church in Ancient Society,* p349.
4 John Chrysostom, *Homilies on 1 Corinthians,* 43.1.
5 John Chrysostom, *Homilies on Colossians,* 7.
6 Ivor Davidson, *A Public Faith. From Constantine to the Medieval World. AD 312-600,* p320.
7 Boniface Ramsey, "Christian Attitudes to Poverty and Wealth" p263. Found in Ian Hazlett (ed.), *Early Christianity. Origins and Evolution to AD 600,* p256-266.

Endnotes

8 Sulpicius Severus, *On the Life of Martin*, 16. Many examples of healings and exorcisms are described throughout this work.
9 Theodoret, *Ecclesiastical History*, 1.23.
10 Sozomen, *Ecclesiastical History*, 5.15.
11 John Chrysostom, *Homilies on Acts*, 18.
12 Augustine, *Sermon* 88.3.
13 Glenn Hinson, *The Evangelization of the Roman Empire*, p275.
14 Kenneth Latourette, *A History of the Expansion of Christianity*, p190-191.
15 Kreider, *The Change of Conversion and the Origin of Christendom*, p56.
16 Hinson, *The Evangelization of the Roman Empire*, p274.
17 Augustine, *Confessions*, 6.
18 Augustine, *Confessions*, 6.3.3.
19 Davidson, *A Public Faith. From Constantine to the Medieval World. AD 312-600*, p248.
20 I am indebted to Victor Schultze, *Geschichte des Untergangs des griechisch-römischen Heidentums*, p322 for the above summary of this poem.
21 Jerome, *Letter*, 57.
22 John 4:39.
23 Augustine, *Tractates on the Gospel of John*, 15.33.
24 Augustine, *Sermon*, 15.
25 Augustine, *First Catechetical Instruction*, 7.
26 Augustine, *First Catechetical Instruction*, 7.
27 Kreider, *The Change of Conversion and the Origin of Christendom*, p57.
28 Augustine, *Sermon*, 15.6.
29 Basil of Caesarea, *Letters*, 164.1.
30 Basil of Caesarea, *Letters*, 164.2.
31 Cyril of Jerusalem, *Catechetical Lectures*, 10.2.
32 Ambrose, *Isaac, or The Soul*, 8.75.
33 Henry Chadwick, *The Church in Ancient Society*, p481.
34 John Chrysostom, *Homily on 1 Corinthians*, 3.9.
35 Caesarius of Arles, *Sermon*, 104.6.
36 Caesarius of Arles, *Sermon*, 104.6.
37 Caesarius of Arles, *Sermon*, 180.1. Cited by Alan Kreider, "Changing Patterns of Conversion in the West," p35. Found in Kreider (ed.), *The Origins of Christendom in the West*, p3-46.
38 William Frend, *The Rise of Christianity*, p704.
39 Michelle Salzman, "Christianity and Paganism, III: Italy", p212. Found in Augustine Cassidy & Frederick Norris, *Cambridge History of Christianity*. Vol. II, p210-230.
40 Salzman, "Christianity and Paganism, III: Italy", p212.
41 Salzman, "Christianity and Paganism, III: Italy", p218 & p221-224.
42 Symnachus, *Letters*, 51.
43 Salzman, "Christianity and Paganism, III: Italy", p216.

44 Michelle Salzman, "How the West was Won: The Christianization of the Roman Aristocracy in the West in the Years after Constantine". Found in Carl Deroux, (ed.) *Studies in Latin Literature and Roman History*, Vol.VI, p451-479.
45 Salzman, "How the West was Won", p465.
46 Salzman, "How the West was Won", p467.
47 Salzman, "Christianity and Paganism, III: Italy" p225.
48 Krieder, "Changing Patterns of Conversion in the West" p29. Found in Krieder (ed.), *The Origins of Christendom in the West*, p3-46. See also Krieder, *The Change of Conversion and the Origin of Christendom*, p69 on this.
49 For example, see the long list of conditions for someone to be admitted to the catechumenate which are spelled out in the *Apostolic Tradition*, 15 & 16.
50 Kreider, *The Change of Conversion and the Origin of Christendom,* p70.
51 Kreider, "Changing Patterns of Conversion in the West", p24-25.
52 Ramsey MacMullen, *Christianizing the Roman Empire,* p80-81.
53 Ramsey MacMullen, *Christianity and Paganism in the 4th – 8th Centuries,* p66-67.
54 Eusebius, *Life of Constantine,* 4.54.
55 Arnold Jones, "The Social Background of the Struggle between Paganism and Christianity". Found in Arnaldo Momigliano, (ed.) *The Conflict Between Paganism and Christianity in the 4th Century*, p17-37. Cited by MacMullen, *Christianizing the Roman Empire*, p58.
56 Luke 14:15-23.
57 Augustine, *Sermons,* 62.8.
58 Edwyn Bevan, *Christianity,* p107.
59 MacMullen, *Christianity and Paganism in the 4th – 8th Centuries,* p12.
60 Sozomen, *Ecclesiastical History,* 2.5.
61 Theodosian Code, 16.10.2. Translation from Brian Croke & Jill Harries, *Religious Conflict in 4th Century Rome*, p19. Cited by Salzman, "Christianity and Paganism, III: Italy", p215.
62 Theodosian Code 16.10.10. Translated by Bart Ehrman & Andrew Jacobs, *Christianity in Late Antiquity 300-450 CE*, p73.
63 Frend, *The Rise of Christianity,* p702-703.
64 Ambrose, *Epistle,* 18.2.
65 This story has been pieced together by MacMullen, *Christianizing the Roman Empire,* p99.
66 Theodosian Code 16.10.19. Cited by MacMullen, *Christianizing the Roman Empire,* p101.
67 Theodosian Code, 16.10.24.
68 Markus, *Christianity in the Roman World,* p123.
69 Libanius, *Oration,* 30, *For the Temples.*
70 Theodoret, *Ecclesiastical History,* 5.29.
71 Theodoret, *Ecclesiastical History,* 5.29.

72 John Chrysostom, *On the Holy Martyr St. Babylas*, 3.
73 Ambrose, *Letter*, 41.27, *To Marcellina*.
74 Ambrose, *Letter*, 41.27, *To Marcellina*.
75 Augsutine, *Sermon*, 24.5-6. Cited by Hinson, *The Evangelization of the Roman Empire*, p63-64.
76 MacMullen, *Christianizing the Roman Empire*, p95.
77 Augustine, *Letter*, 50.
78 Caesarius of Arles, *Sermon*, 142.2. Cited by Kreider, *The Change of Conversion and the Origin of Christendom*, p72.
79 Origen, *Against Celsus*, 3.55.
80 Kreider, *The Change of Conversion and the Origin of Christendom*, p72-73.
81 MacMullen, *Christianizing the Roman Empire*, p95.
82 Mark the Deacon, *Life of Porphyry*, 40.
83 Mark the Deacon, *Life of Porphyry*, 41.
84 *Codex Justinian*, 1.11. Cited by Charles Robinson, *The Conversion of Europe*, p236.
85 John of Ephesus, *Ecclesiastical History*, 3.27.
86 Chadwick, *The Church in Ancient Society*, p349.
87 Salzman, "Christianity and Paganism, III: Italy," p229.
88 Maximus of Turin, *Sermons*, 107. Cited by Lizzi, R. "Ambrose's Contemporaries and the Christianisation of Northern Italy," p168. Found in *The Journal of Roman Studies*, Vol.80, p156-173.
89 Maximus of Turin, *Sermons*, 91.2 and 107. Cited by MacMullen, *Christianizing the Roman Empire*, p65.
90 Caesarius of Arles, *Sermon* 53.2. Cited by Kreider, *The Change of Conversion and the Origin of Christendom*, p72.
91 Gregory the Great, *Epistles*, 4.26.
92 Eusebius, *Life of Constantine*, 3.66.
93 Libanius, *Pro Templis-Oration*, 30.10.
94 Lizzi, "Ambrose's Contemporaries and the Christianisation of Northern Italy", p173.
95 Markus, *Christianity in the Roman World*, p104.
96 Chadwick, *The Church in Ancient Society*, p321.
97 Davidson, *A Public Faith. From Constantine to the Medieval World. AD 312-600*, p255.
98 Frend, *The Rise of Christianity*, p559.
99 Augustine, *Confessions*, 9.6.14.
100 Davidson, *A Public Faith. From Constantine to the Medieval World. AD 312-600*, p267.
101 Davidson, *A Public Faith. From Constantine to the Medieval World. AD 312-600*, p256.
102 Marc-Antoine Kugener, *Vie De Sévère Par Jean de Beith-Aphthonia*, p244. Cited by MacMullen, *Christianizing the Roman Empire*, p147, footnote 6.

103 Bradshaw, "The Effects of the Coming of Christendom on Early Christian Worship," p275. Found in Kreider (ed.), *The Origins of Christendom in the West,* p269-286.
104 Aidan Kavanagh, *On Liturgical Theology,* p65. Kavanagh describes these parades as "Worship on the town".
105 Bradshaw, "The Effects of the Coming of Christendom on Early Christian Worship," p274.
106 Basil of Caesarea, *Homilies on Hexaemeron,* 8.8.
107 Basil of Caesarea, *Homilies on Hexaemeron,* 8.8.
108 Dale Irvin & Scott Sunquist, *History of the World Christian Movement,* Vol.1, p163.
109 Augustine, *First Catechetical Instruction,* 7.
110 Cyril of Jerusalem, *Procatechesis,* 5.
111 Kreider, *The Change of Conversion and the Origin of Christendom,* p41.
112 Kreider, *The Change of Conversion and the Origin of Christendom,* p41.
113 Caesarius of Arles, *Sermon,* 78.1.
114 Stephen the Deacon, *Life of Caesarius,* 1.27. Translated by William Klingshirn, *Caesarius of Arles: Life, Testament, Letters,* p22.
115 Stephen the Deacon, *Life of Caesarius,* 1.27. Translated by Klingshirn, *Caesarius of Arles: Life, Testament, Letters,* p22.
116 Davidson, *A Public Faith. From Constantine to the Medieval World. AD 312-600,* p320.
117 Martin of Braga, *Unchastising the Simple Folk (De Correctione Rusticorum),* 16.
118 Martin of Braga, *Unchastising the Simple Folk (De Correctione Rusticorum),* 17.
119 Basil of Caesarea, *Letters,* 88.
120 Basil of Caesarea, *Letters,* 104, 284-5 & 110 respectively. These citations are collected by Chadwick, *The Church in Ancient Society,* p342.
121 MacMullen, *Christianity and Paganism in the Fourth to Eight Centuries,* p11.
122 Chadwick, *The Church in Ancient Society,* p342. Based on a study of several of Basil's letters.
123 Chadwick, *The Church in Ancient Society,* p309.
124 Irvin & Sunquist, *History of the World Christian Movement,* Vol.I, p224-225.
125 Venantius Fortunatus, *Carm.* 3.14. Cited by Winrich Lohr, "Western Christianities," p36. Found in Augustine Casidy & Frederick Norris, *The Cambridge History of Christianity,* Vol. II, p39-51.
126 Davidson, *A Public Faith. From Constantine to the Medieval World. AD 312-600,* p281.
127 http://en.wikipedia.org/wiki/philastrius Retrieved 14/10/2011.
128 Abraames is briefly mentioned in Theodoret, *Ecclesiastical History,* 4.25. but most of the following information about him comes from Alban Butler & Charles Butler, *The Lives of the Primitive Fathers, Martyrs and other*

Principal Saints: Compiled from Original Monuments and other Authentic Records. Vol.2. 3rd Edition.
129 Butler & Butler, *The Lives of the Primitive Fathers, Martyrs and other Principal Saints: Compiled from Original Monuments and other Authentic Records.* Vol.2. 3rd Edition, p158.
130 Schultze, *Geschichte des Untergangs des griechisch-romischen Heidentums*, p318. Translation mine.
131 Frend, *The Rise of Christianity,* p709.
132 Frend, *The Rise of Christianity,* p708. Citing various French language sources.
133 Ian Wood, *The Missionary Life*, p6.
134 Butterfield, *Christianity and History*, p135.

CHAPTER 4
1   William Frend, *The Early Church*, p189.
2   William Frend, *Town and Country in the Early Christian Centuries*, Chapter X, "The Failure of the Persecutions in the Roman Empire," p283.
3   Frederick Norris, "Greek Christianities," p110. Found in Casiday & Norris, (eds.), *The Cambridge History of Christianity*, Vol. II, p70-117.
4   Henry Chadwick, *The Early Church*, p176.
5   Ivor Davidson, *A Public Faith. From Constantine to the Medieval World. AD 312-600,* p136-137.
6   Matthew 18:3. These examples are cited by Peter King, *Western Monasticism*, p54.
7   *Historia Monachorum in Aegypto (History of the Egyptian Monks).* Prologue.
8   Columba Stewart, "Monasticism", p349. Found in Esler, *The Early Christian World.* Vol. 1, p344-366.
9   *Historia Monachorum in Aegypto (History of the Egyptian Monks)*, 21.
10 *Historia Monachorum in Aegypto (History of the Egyptian Monks)*, 21.
11 Palladius, *Lausiac History*, 7.4.
12 *The Rule of St. Benedict*, 53.
13 *Shorter Rules of St Basil*, 207. Cited by Marilyn Dunn, *The Emergence of Monasticism*, p38.
14 Palladius, *Lausiac History*, 32.9.
15 William Frend, *Martyrdom and Persecution in the Early Church*, p462.
16 Palladius, *Lausiac History*, 32.10.
17 John Cassian, *Institutes*, 10.22.
18 Samuel Rubenson, "Asceticism and Monasticism, I: Eastern", p665. Found in Casiday & Norris (eds.), *The Cambridge History of Christianity*, Vol. II, p637-668.
19 Robert Markus, *The End of Ancient Christianity,* p199.
20 Rubenson, "Asceticism and Monasticism, I: Eastern" p661.
21 Sozomen, *Ecclesiastical History,* 6.27.
22 Sozomen, *Ecclesiastical History,* 6.27.

23 William Davidson, *A Public Faith. From Constantine to the Medieval World. AD 312-600*, p139.
24 Frend, *Religion Popular and Unpopular in the Early Christian Centuries*, Chapter XVII "The Monks and the Survival of the East Roman Empire in the Fifth Century", p13.
25 Norris, "Greek Christianities," p110.
26 Frederick Foakes-Jackson, *History of the Christian Church to AD 461*, p564f.
27 John Meyendorff, *Imperial Unity and Christian Division*, p96.
28 This dynamic is discussed in more detail in Barnes, "Constantine and the Christians of Persia". *The Journal of Roman Studies*. Vol. 75, (1985) p126-136. There is an interesting (and tragic) parallel here with the fate of indigenous Christians in present-day Iraq who, during and after the US led invasion of 2003, found themselves identified with the invaders even though Christians have been present in Iraq for at least 1500 years.
29 *Odes of Solomon*, 6.8-6.11.
30 Meyendorff, *Imperial Unity and Christian Division*, p100.
31 Most of what is known about Alopen comes from a large black stone stele which was unearthed near the modern city of Xi'Am in the early seventeenth century. The full text can be found in P. Yoshio Saeki, *The Nestorian Documents and Relics in China*. Summaries of its contents are quoted in Dale Irvin & Scott Sunquist, *History of the World Christian Movement*, p316-317 and Dennis Hickley, *The First Christians of China*, p10-11.
32 Hickley *The First Christians of China*, p11. Citing Arthur Moule, *Christians in China Before the Year 1500*, p38-39.
33 This summary of Ulfilas' life and ministry is largely taken from Richard Fletcher, *The Conversion of Europe*, p72-74.
34 Philostorgius, *Ecclesiastical History*, 2.5; Socrates, *Ecclesiastical History*, 4.33; Sozomen, *Ecclesiastical History*, 6.37.
35 Sozomen, *Ecclesiastical History*, 6.37.
36 Basil, *Letter to Ascholius*, 2.
37 For a chapter length assessment of the sources (reliable and unreliable) which we have for St. Patrick see Richard Hanson, *St. Patrick: His Origins and Career*, p72-105.
38 Patrick, *Confession*, 61.
39 Patrick, *Confession*, 40. The Bible references quoted are Matthew 4:19, Luke 6:17 & Matthew 28:19-20. He goes on to quote many more similar passages.
40 Richard Fletcher, *The Conversion of Europe*, p86.
41 Patrick, *Confession*, 37.
42 Edward Thompson, *Who was St. Patrick?*, p79.
43 Patrick, *Confession*, 53.
44 Patrick, *Confession*, 52.
45 Patrick, *Confession*, 41.

46 Glenn Hinson, *The Evangelisation of the Roman Empire*, p278.
47 Richard Hanson, *The Life and Writings of St. Patrick*, p33.
48 Patrick, *Confession*, 51.
49 Patrick, *Confession*, 52.
50 George Hunter, *The Celtic Way of Evangelism*, p21.
51 Davidson, *A Public Faith*, p357.
52 Patrick, *Confession*, 6.
53 Dana Robert, *Christian Mission, How Christianity Became a World Religion*, p150.
54 Dáithí Ó hÓgáin, *The Sacred Isle. Belief and Religion in Pre-Christian Ireland*, p192. In fact, p184-202 of Ó hÓgáin's book details further insights into the religion of pagan Ireland or discerns aspects of religious beliefs in pagan Ireland from Patrick's preaching which clearly implies that Patrick really attempted to engage relevantly with his listeners.
55 Patrick, *Confession*, 60.
56 Neill, *A History of Christian Missions*, p56.
57 A recent and comprehensive summary biography of Columba's life is provided by Richard Sharpe in the introduction to his translation of Adomnan, *Life of Saint Columba*, p1-98.
58 Bede, *Ecclesiastical History of the English Nation*, 3.4.
59 Adomnan, *Life of Saint Columba*, Second Preface.
60 Brendan is one famous example of this, as is Columbanus whose travels will be considered in more detail later.
61 Fletcher, *The Conversion of Europe*, p94.
62 Frend, *The Rise of Christianity*, p879.
63 Cited by Sharpe, translation of the *Life of Saint Columba* by Adomnan, p31.
64 Fletcher, *The Conversion of Europe*, p95.
65 Adomnan, *Life of Saint Columba*, 3.14.
66 Fletcher, *The Conversion of Europe*, p94.
67 Bede, *Ecclesiastical History of the English Nation*, 3.5.
68 Bede, *Ecclesiastical History of the English Nation*, 3.5.
69 Bede, *Ecclesiastical History of the English Nation*, 3.5.
70 David Adam, *Aidan, Bede, Cuthbert*, p49.
71 Bede, *Ecclesiastical History of the English Nation*, 3.3.
72 Bede, *Ecclesiastical History of the English Nation*, 3.5.
73 Bede, *Ecclesiastical History of the English Nation*, 3.3.
74 Most of this summary of Columbanus' life comes from Frend, *The Rise of Christianity*, p880. For a longer account of his life see Tomas O'Fiaich, *Columbanus in his Own Words*. Also, see the *Life of Columbanus* written by Jonas, a monk at Bobbio, around 643 AD, just a few decades after Columbanus' death.
75 Ian Wood, *The Missionary Life*, p34.
76 Jonas of Bobbio, *Life of Columbanus*, 37.
77 Jonas of Bobbio, *Life of Columbanus*, 56.

78　Dunn, *The Emergence of Monasticism,* p159.
79　Jonas of Bobbio, *Life of Columbanus,* 51.
80　Jonas of Bobbio, *Life of Columbanus,* 53. Italics Mine.
81　Jonas of Bobbio, *Life of Columbanus,* 10.
82　Jonas of Bobbio, *Life of Columbanus,* 11.
83　Fletcher, *The Conversion of Europe,* p96.
84　Hinson, *The Evangelization of the Roman Empire,* p279.
85　Bruce Shelley, *Church History in Plain Language,* p156.
86　Jonas of Bobbio, *Life of Columbanus,* 17.
87　Diana Leatham, *They Built on Rock,* p168.
88　Brendan Lehane, *Early Celtic Christianity,* p151.
89　Lehane, *Early Celtic Christianity,* p152.
90　Jonas of Bobbio, *Life of Columbanus,* 11.
91　Lehane, *Early Celtic Christianity,* p154.
92　Lehane, *Early Celtic Christianity,* p154.
93　Lehane, *Early Celtic Christianity,* p159.
94　Bede, *Ecclesiastical History of the English Nation,* 1.23.
95　Jocelyn Hillgarth, *The Conversion of Western Europe,* p111.
96　Gregory, *Homiliae in Hiezechielem,* 1.3.7. Cited by Robert Markus, *Gregory the Great and his World,* p186.
97　Bede, *Ecclesiastical History of the English Nation,* 1.25.
98　Bede, *Ecclesiastical History of the English Nation,* 1.25.
99　Gregory the Great, *Epistles,* 8.30.
100　Chadwick, *The Early Church,* p256.
101　Bede, *Ecclesiastical History of the English Nation,* 1.26.
102　Gregory the Great, *Epistles,* 11.29.
103　Markus, *The End of Ancient Christianity,* p182.
104　Gregory the Great, *Epistles,* 11.66.
105　This letter is recorded in Bede, *Ecclesiastical History of the English Nation,* 1.30.
106　Ian Wood, "The Mission of Augustine of Canterbury to the English". *Speculum.* Vol. 69.1 (1994), p12.
107　Bede, *Ecclesiastical History of the English Nation,* 1.26.
108　Markus, *Gregory the Great and his World,* p184.
109　Meyendorff, *Imperial Unity and Christian Division,* p95.
110　Latourette, *The First Five Centuries,* p226-227.
111　Rufinus, *Ecclesiastical History,* 1.10. Rufinus translated Eusebius' *Ecclesiastical History* into Latin but combined Eusebius' ninth and tenth books and then added two further books himself resulting in an eleven book Church History in Latin.
112　Rufinus, *Ecclesiastical History,* 10.11.
113　Cited by Moffett, *A History of Christianity in Asia,* p275 and Samuel Meyendorff, *Imperial Unity and Christian Division,* p111-112.

Endnotes

114 Bundy, "Early Asian and East African Christianities", p142. Found in Casiday and Norris (eds.), *The Cambridge History of Christianity,* Vol. II, p118-144.
115 Bardaisan, *Book of the Laws*. Cited by Moffett, *A History of Christianity in Asia,* p207.
116 David Bundy, "Early Asian and East African Christianities," p143.
117 This document is summarised by Alphonse Mingana, "Early Spread of Christianity in Central Asia and the Far East: A New Document" *Bulletin of the John Rylands Library,* Vol. IX, Number 2, (July 1925), p303ff.
118 *Chronicle of Seert,* 7.128. Cited by Mingana, "Early Spread of Christianity in Central Asia and the Far East: A New Document" and Moffett, *A History of Christianity in Asia,* p208-209.
119 The above summary of this story is largely taken from Bengt Sundkler & Christopher Steed, *A History of the Church in Africa,* p34-35 and Meyendorff, *Imperial Unity and Christian Division,* p118-119.
120 Elizabeth Isichei, *A History of Christianity in Africa,* p33.
121 Irvin & Sunquist, *History of the World Christian Movement,* p217.
122 Irvin & Sunquist, *History of the World Christian Movement,* p218.
123 Irvin & Sunquist, *History of the World Christian Movement,* p250.
124 This story is told by John of Ephesus in his *Ecclesiastical History*. My summary is based on William Frend "The Mission to Nubia," found in Frend, *Town and Country in the Early Christian Centuries XXII.* p10-16; Irvin & Sunquist, *History of the World Christian Movement,* p250-251; Sundkler & Steed, *A History of the Church in Africa,* p30-31.
125 Fletcher, *The Conversion of Europe,* p67.
126 The area between the Aegean Sea and Black Sea today covering parts of south-eastern Bulgaria, north-eastern Greece and the European part of Turkey.
127 Sozomen, *Ecclesiastical History,* 2.6.
128 Philostorgius, *Ecclesiastical History,* 2.5. "Scythians" refers to inhabitants of a huge area north of the Black Sea and the Caspian Sea covering large parts of modern day Ukraine and Kazakhstan. "Ister" refers to the river which is now called the Danube.
129 Prosper of Aquitaine, *The Call of all Nations,* 2.33.
130 Translation found in an article entitled "St. Palladius" in the *Catholic Encyclopaedia* at www.newadvent.org.
131 Hanson, *St. Patrick his Origins and Career,* p54.
132 Wood, *The Missionary Life,* p7.
133 From Tacitus' Memoir of his father-in-law Agricola cited by Fletcher, *The Conversion of Europe,* p80.
134 Fletcher, *The Conversion of Europe,* p81.
135 Kenneth Latourette, *The Expansion of Christianity,* p221.
136 Fletcher, *The Conversion of Europe,* p81.

CHAPTER 5

1. As per the *Theodosian Code* discussed in Chapter Three.
2. In the following pages the term 'Western world' will be used to reference these parts of the world, namely Europe and other continents which were largely populated by migrating Europeans at the expense of their indigenous populations, such as North America and Australasia.
3. Stephen Skuce, *Faith Reborn: Mission in a (Wonderfully) Strange New Ireland*, p10.
4. Skuce, *Faith Reborn: Mission in a (Wonderfully) Strange New Ireland*, p10.
5. John Joseph Lee, *Ireland, 1912-1985: Politics and Society*, p657.
6. https://alphahistory.com/northernireland/ulster-covenant-1912. Retrieved 13/5/2021.
7. Jonathan Bardon, *A History of Ulster*, p538-9.
8. https://www.irishtimes.com/news/politics/marriage-referendum/ireland-becomes-first-country-to-approve-same-sex-marriage-by-popular-vote-1.2223646. Retrieved 29/4/2021.
9. Fraser Hosford, *Down With This Sort of Thing*, p20.
10. https://www.rte.ie/news/2011/0720/303925-cloyne. Retrieved 3/5/2021.
11. Barna, *Finding Faith in Ireland*, p28.
12. https://ionainstitute.ie/wp-content/uploads/2014/11/Iona_Religious_knowledge_pollApr07.pdf. Retrieved 10/5/2021.
13. Cited by Honsberger in a research paper entitled "How to Reach a Pagan World". http://emnr.org/papers/how_to_reach_a_pagan_world.htm. Retrieved 10/11/2011.
14. Stuart Murray, *Post-Christendom*, p19.
15. Murray, *Post-Christendom*, p20.
16. Howard Lewis of "Evangelical Ministries" in Belfast. "Christian Living in a Twenty-first Century Pluralist Society". Unpublished lecture.
17. Michael Frost & Alan Hirsch, *The Shaping of Things to Come*, p18.
18. Murray, *Post-Christendom*, p9.
19. Murray, *Post-Christendom*, p231-2.
20. Frost & Hirsch, *The Shaping of Things to Come*, p15.
21. Augustine, *The City of God*, 5.24.
22. Kevin Hargaden, "Thinking Theologically about Rights". *VOX Magazine*, Jan-March 2017, p13.
23. John Finney, *Finding Faith Today*, p68.
24. On p68, Finney mentions three other pieces of research that preceded his, conducted independently by Gavin Reid, John Finney and the Methodist Church in Britain during the 1980's which gave figures of 13%, 11% and 5% respectively for the percentage of new converts to Christianity for whom a large evangelistic event was the main factor. Unfortunately, Finney does not cite further biographical details for these earlier studies.
25. Kieran Beville, *Preaching Christ in a Post-Modern Culture*, p12.
26. Finney, *Finding Faith Today*, p25. Italics mine.

27　Stuart Murray, *Church After Christendom*, p156.
28　Murray, *Church After Christendom*, p156.
29　Hugh Halter & Matt Smay, *The Tangible Kingdom*, p55.
30　Murray, *Church After Christendom*, p156.
31　Murray, *Post Christendom*, p230.
32　Finney, *Finding Faith Today*, p47.
33　See chapter 4 of Finney, *Finding Faith Today* for detailed figures.
34　Lewis, "Christian Living in a Twenty-first Century Pluralist Society". Unpublished lecture.
35　Howard Lewis, "Key Words for Twenty-First Evangelism". Article in *Frontiers* magazine, p17-19.
36　Mark 1:17.
37　Frost & Hirsch, *The Shaping of Things to Come*, p57.
38　Eric Swanson, "Ten Paradigm Shifts Towards Community Transformation," p1. Published online by Hill Consulting Group at www.hillconsultinggroup.org/resources.php. Retrieved 16/10/2011.
39　Matthew 5:13-16.
40　Unpublished talk given at Faithworks Conference, Eastbourne, 5th November 2005.
41　Cray et. al., *Mission-Shaped Church*, p37. Based on Philip Richter & Leslie Francis, *Gone but not Forgotten*.
42　Information quantifying the relevant size of each group in Ireland is not available to the best of my knowledge.
43　*Growing and Vibrant. A Census and Survey of Christian Churches beyond the Traditional Four Main Denominations.* EAI. Dublin 2018.
44　https://www.irishtimes.com/news/education/baptisms-remain-popular-as-mass-attendance-declines-1.2448687. Retrieved 28/4/2021.
45　https://www.irishtimes.com/news/education/baptisms-remain-popular-as-mass-attendance-declines-1.2448687. Retrieved 28/4/2021.
46　Barna, *Finding Faith in Ireland,* p12.
47　Murray, *Post-Christendom*, p9.
48　Murray, *Post-Christendom*, p10.
49　Halter & Smay, *The Tangible Kingdom*, p72.
50　Murray, *Post-Christendom*, p85.
51　Frost & Hirsch, *The Shaping of Things to Come*, p48-49.
52　John Finney, *Recovering the Past*, p141.
53　Philip McKinley, "Pitch His Tent". Unpublished Interim Report on the Development of Ashtown Methodist. p2.
54　McKinley, "Pitch His Tent", Unpublished Interim Report on the Development of Ashtown Methodist. p10.
55　Finney, *Finding Faith Today*, p23.
56　Cray et.al., *Mission-Shaped Church*, p41.
57　Lausanne Committee for World Evangelisation, "The Local Church in Mission: Becoming a Missional Congregation in the Twenty-first Century

Global Context and the Opportunities Offered Through Tent Making Ministry." Lausanne Occasional Paper, Number 39, Section 2.1.
58 Gerhard Lohfink, *Jesus and Community*, p137.

CHAPTER 6

1   For more stories similar to those I will tell here, readers should refer to *Gloriously Ordinary* by Ruth Garvey-Williams et al.
2   Ruth Garvey Williams et al., *Gloriously Ordinary*, p84.
3   Acts 2:46.
4   Rich Villodas, *The Deeply Formed Life*, p189ff.
5   Rosaria Butterfield, *The Gospel Comes with a House Key*, p12.
6   Brian Sanders, Ross Hill & Simon Kilpatrick introduce and discuss this idea on the November 2021 edition of the *Mission Disco* podcast, https://podtail.com/en/podcast/mission-disco/november-episode-the-nature-of-work. Retrieved 9/12/21.
7   https://ireland.cityofsanctuary.org/sanctuary-in-faith. Retrieved 29/8/2021.
8   https://onustraining.co.uk/safe-church. Retrieved 29/8/2021.
9   Graham Johnston, *Preaching to a Post-Modern World*, p104.
10 Eddie Gibbs, *Church Morph*, p43.
11 For example, 1 Peter 2:12.
12 Robert Plummer, *Paul's Understanding of the Church's Mission*, p30-31.
13 Eckhard Schnabel, *Paul the Missionary*, p195.
14 Paul Bowers, "Church and Mission in Paul", *Journal for the Study of the New Testament*. Vol 44 (1991) p89-111. p101.
15 Finney, *Recovering the Past – Celtic and Roman Missions*, p127.
16 Michael Green, *Evangelism in the Early Church*, p178.
17 Robert Wilken, *The Christians as the Romans Saw Them*, p63-64.
18 Ramsey MacMullen, *Christianizing the Roman Empire*, p28.
19 Wilken, *The Christians as the Romans Saw Them*, p63.
20 Green, *Evangelism in the Early Church*, pXVII.
21 Joel Edwards, *An Agenda for Change*, chapter 2.
22 Hugh Halter & Matt Smay, *The Tangible Kingdom*, p54.
23 Kretchmar, "Christian Life and Mission of the Early Church," p94-128 in Heinzgünter Frohmes *et.al.*, *Kirchengeschichte als Missionsgeschichte*, p123 (Translation mine).
24 Raymond Fung, *The Isaiah Vision*, p17.
25 Fung, *The Isaiah Vision*, p14.
26 Rev. John Woodside unpublished lecture to Methodist Ministers. Roscrea, Co. Tipperary. November 1998.
27 Joel Edwards, "Urban Mission." Unpublished lecture delivered in Cork. January 2011.
28 1 Peter 3:15.
29 Lewis, "Key Words for Twenty-First Evangelism". Article in Frontiers magazine, p17.

30. Frost & Hirsch, *The Shaping of Things to Come,* p58.
31. Ephesians 4:12.
32. Murray, *Post-Christendom*, p229.
33. Stephen Croft unpublished lecture to Methodist Ministers in Sligo. January 2007.
34. Bob Roxburgh, "What is the Missional Church?" Unpublished Paper.
35. 1 Peter 3:15.
36. Edwards, *An Agenda for Change,* expands on this theme in chapter 9.
37. Halter & Smay, *The Tangible Kingdom,* p46.
38. Henri Daniel & Yvan Godon "France a Missionary Land?" Translated in Malasie Ward & Cardinal Griffin, *France Pagan? The Mission of Abbe Godin*, p166.
39. Daniel & Godon, "France a Missionary Land?", p165.
40. Christian Schwarz, *Natural Church Development*, p29.
41. Finney, *Recovering the Past*, p45.
42. Edwyn Bevan, *Christianity,* p51.
43. Bishop Sifredo Teixeira, speaking at Methodist Church in Britain Pre-Conference Consultation with international Partners, 22-23 June 2021. Italics mine.
44. Eric Swanson, "Ten Paradigm Shifts Toward Community Transformation," p4. Published online by Hill Consulting Group at www.hillconsultinggroup.org/resources.php. Retrieved 16/10/2011.
45. Frost & Hirsch, *The Shaping of Things to Come,* p57.
46. Michael Frost, *The Road to Missional,* p28.
47. Vincent Donovan, *Christianity Rediscovered*, p18.
48. Skuce, *Faith Reborn: Mission in a (Wonderfully) Strange New Ireland,* p99.
49. Skuce, *Faith Reborn: Mission in a (Wonderfully) Strange New Ireland,* p99.
50. Brendan Lehane, *Early Celtic Christianity,* p188.
51. John 10:10.
52. Luke 4:18-19.
53. https://renovare.org/podcast/dallas-willard-living-the-divine-conspiracy. Retrieved 10/9/2021.
54. Barna, *Finding Faith in Ireland*, p55.
55. Good News Bible.
56. Ronnie Wilson, 1979. Thankyou Music.
57. For more on this theme see Chapter 3 of *Gloriously Ordinary* by Ruth Garvey-Williams et al.
58. 2 Corinthians 5:14.

CONCLUSION
1. John 1:14
2. Ian Gibson "The Methodist Newsletter", Vol. 49, No 536, December 2021, p17.

3   Luke 22:27
4   The Right Reverend Ronald Bowlby. http://npbc.uk.com/pdfs-5min/Christianity%20in%20Britain%20in%20the%2020th%20century.pdf. Retrieved 1/11/2021
5   Philippians 2:7